Second Edition

- by -

Michael A. Aquino, Ph.D.
Lt. Colonel, Psychological Operations (Ret.)
United States Army

ISBN-13:
978-1535199568

ISBN-10:
1535199563

Books by Michael A. Aquino

[all available in both printed and Kindle ebook editions]

Non-Fiction

The Church of Satan (2 Volumes)
Extreme Prejudice:
    The Presidio "Satanic Abuse" Scam
IlluminAnX: Rosicrucianism Reawakened
<u>The MindWar Trilogy</u>
    MindWar
    MindStar
    FindFar
The Neutron Bomb
The Temple of Set (2 Volumes)

Fiction

FireForce: A Star Wars *Parody*
    Including: Secret of the Lost Ark
Morlindalë: Song of Illuminate Darkness
    - by "The One Ring"
Ode to Esmé: Memoirs of Captain Nemo
We Break the Sword: The Nazi Peace of 1940

Autobiographical

Ghost Rides
    Including: *Grail Mission*

Edited

Pegasus in Pinfeathers: Collected Poems 1919-1928
    - by Betty Ford

To:

Colonel John B. Alexander, USA
Isaac Asimov, Ph.D.
Alex Burns
David Carradine
Paddy Chayefsky
General Wesley K. Clark, USA
José M.R. Delgado, M.D.
Walt Disney
Paul Draper
Commander Ian Fleming, RNVR
C/Colonel Susan Foss, USA
John Fowles
Michael R. Gordon, Ph.D.
Raghavan Iyer, D.Phil.
Henry Jones, Jr., Ph.D.
Paul Kantner
Colonel Robert H. Kies, USA
Nikolai Dmitriyevich Kondratiev
Paul Krassner
Dennis Kucinich
Major General Edward G. Lansdale, USAF
Bruce Lee
John C. Lilly, M.D.
Perry London, Ph.D.

Niccolò Machiavelli
Michael Murphy
Ralph Nader
George Orwell
Peter D. Ouspensky
General George S. Patton, Jr., USA
Colonel L. Fletcher Prouty, USAF
Sidney Reilly
Kathryn Leigh Scott
Captain Dale Seago, USA
Grace Slick
Colonel John P. Spickelmier, USA
Oliver Stone
Colonel Richard L. Sutter, USA
Thomas Szasz, M.D.
Mark Thornally
Mark Twain
USSPACECOM J2X/MJ
Major General Paul E. Vallely, USA
Jules Verne
Peter Viereck, Ph.D.
H.G. Wells

Every gun that is made, every warship launched, every rocket fired signifies, in the final sense, a theft from those who hunger and are not fed, those who are cold and not clothed. This world in arms is not spending money alone. It is spending the sweat of its laborers, the genius of its scientists, the hopes of its children. This is not a way of life at all in any true sense. Under the cloud of threatening war, it is humanity hanging from a cross of iron.

- Dwight D. Eisenhower

Table of Contents

Foreword

- by Gregory S. Seese, Psy.D.
       Major, Psychological Operations, U.S. Army

> The mind is its own place, and in itself
> can make a heaven of hell, a hell of heaven.
>   - John Milton, *Paradise Lost*

The concept of MindWar (MW) represents a holistic and pro-active approach to Psychological Operations (PSYOP), rather than the traditional reactionary role to which it's been relegated. MW focuses on emerging and anticipating problems, situations, and conditions affecting the Information Environment (IE) not only to manage the perceptions of groups and individuals, but to address the conditions and situations that fuel discontent and drive instability. Targeting only the symptoms of a problem, rather than addressing the underlying causes and conditions, results in only a temporary and short-term solution. This shortsighted approach has proven costly, has limited effectiveness, and does not bring about nor foster long-term change.

MW provides the capability to resolve problems **before** they begin. Utilizing 21st century scientifically-valid, empirically-based methodologies, MW is the equivalent of a mental preemptive strike. To be effective,

MW requires a detailed analysis of an anticipated or emerging situation, focusing on the physical, information, and cognitive domains. Only this combined approach will result in a necessary understanding of the underlying issues that need to be addressed for MW effectiveness.

MW can be used to address not only traditional problems such as war and conflict, but also the full range of asymmetric threats (terrorism, violent extremism, drug and human trafficking), the challenges associated with globalization (migration, spread of disease, overpopulation), and the social and economic problems resulting from the physical effects of climate change (crop failure, economic volatility, and resource competition).

MW further has the potential to support the major end states of the Strategic Framework for Stabilization and Reconstruction[1]   outlined by the US Institute of Peace that were adopted by the U.S. Army Peacekeeping and Stability Operations Institute for use in the conduct of civil military operations. These end states were framed according to the perception of the host nation population, as they will be the final arbiters of whether peace has been achieved.

This book proposes a conceptual and operational design for the development of a MW capability.   It discusses a pragmatic, multiphase model as the framework for its execution, and reviews a body of research conducted over the last 30 years that exemplifies creative and out-of-the-box thinking.

---

[1]   United States Institute for Peace and United States Army Peacekeeping and Stability Operations Institute, *Guiding Principles for Stabilization and Reconstruction*. Washington, D.C.: Endowment of the United States Institute for Peace, 2009.

Gregory S. Seese most recently served as the J5 Director of Plans at the Joint Information Support Task Force - Special Operations, U.S. Special Operations Command Central. Previously he spent several years at the John F. Kennedy Special Warfare Center & School at Fort Bragg, North Carolina as the PSYOP Advanced Individual Training Company Commander, Course Manager of the PSYOP Officer Qualification Course, and Chief of the PSYOP Training Branch.

Major Seese served in Bosnia-Herzegovina and in Operation Enduring Freedom with the 3rd and 19th Special Forces Groups. His research interests include attitude and behavior change, motivation, deception, behavioral prediction/modeling, and bio & neurofeedback.

Major Seese is a licensed psychologist and has a Bachelor of Arts, Master of Science, and Doctorate in Psychology. He also earned a graduate certificate in Stability, Security, and Development in Complex Operations from the Naval Post Graduate School.

Preface

> Politicians should read science fiction,
> not westerns and detective stories.
> - Arthur C. Clarke

Since the first caveman beaned another one with a rock, violence against the bodies and belongings of others (hereinafter "PhysWar"/PW) has been a constant and until now accepted method of addressing, if not resolving disputes between tribes, feudal holdings, and eventually nation-states. Indeed PW has been glorified and its participants honored, despite its being an engine of death, destruction, and misery. Certainly no other human pastime has been more publicized and memorialized in literature and the arts. A visit to any library or museum is sufficient to demonstrate that, despite all rhetoric to the contrary, humanity loves the mystique of **war**.

The problem with this addiction is not merely one of compassion for PW's victims. If PW had a record of positive accomplishment - resolving the issues that prompted it - it could at least be excused on these grounds.[2] But this is rarely, indeed almost never the case.

---

[2] In Italy for 30 years under the Borgias they had warfare, terror, murder, and bloodshed, but they produced Michelangelo, Leonardo da Vinci, and the Renaissance. In Switzerland they had brotherly love - they had 500 years of democracy and peace, and what did that produce? The cuckoo clock. - Harry Lime, *The Third Man*, 1949

The moment that cooperative, reasoned dialogue is discarded in favor of brute force, the inexorable tendency is to reject anything other than that blind force henceforth. Negotiation, compromise, and rational problem-solving are abandoned, indeed condemned as signs of weakness and betrayal.

As humanity has advanced technologically, the weapons of PW have become more efficient, projectable, and lethal. But whether it is an industrial nation with armed forces deployed worldwide, or guerrilla conflicts [the currently-in-vogue term is "terrorism"] using hand-to-hand combat, the allure has not slackened in the least. Humanity still craves, and loves, war.[3]

The 21st-century dilemma for the United States is simply that PW is no longer practical on the scale it now requires to be effective, if the destruction or exhaustion of another country, or intra/transnational group of people, can be considered effective. With the explosion of world population and corresponding migration, there are now too many enemies, whether individual or institutional. PW against them can no longer be neatly confined to national boundaries or the traditional taking of token-cities. And PW has become ruinously expensive, especially for the United States as the world's *de facto* policeman and preeminent warfare state.

Indeed it is arguable that war and world-policing have become **the** *raison d'être* of the United States. The Department of Defense (DOD), which absorbs approximately one-quarter of the entire U.S. Government

---

[3] Like Harry Lime, Friedrich Nietzsche (1844-1900) regarded war as an energizing, revitalizing political influence, deterring the otherwise sluggish descent towards the "last man". But he did not love war for its destructiveness: "And perhaps a great day will come when a people, distinguished through war and victories, voluntarily proclaims: 'We break the sword.' Disarming oneself, from an **intensity** of feeling, while one is the best armed: That is the means to **real** peace." (*The Wanderer and his Shadow*, 1880).

budget, has long since abandoned its titular mission of defending the territorial United States, so much so that an entirely new Government Department - Homeland Security - has been created for that purpose.[4] Rather it is DOD's function to project U.S. military power into the territories and affairs of other countries. The stated justifications are many: "democracy", "weapons of mass destruction", "nuclear nonproliferation", "regional stability", "anti-terrorism" (replacing "anti-communism"), and/or the catchall "U.S. national security".

Not only has the United States assumed the role of world policeman, but the planet's other countries generally take this role for granted. Every new crisis, especially of a violent nature, generates an appeal for U.S. intervention, or at least expectation of it.

Assuming that mankind's lust for war cannot be eliminated - the League of Nations and its United Nations successor stand as utopian monuments to failure in this naïve desire - what can realistically be done about it?

The answer is that while war will remain inevitable and inexorable, it is both possible and practical to revise the way it is conducted. As the world's policeman and supreme warfare state, the United States has a unique prerogative to determine and change the context and structure of present and future war. It is to this problem - and opportunity - that this book speaks.

The new type of war proposed here allows subnational groups, nation-states, and multinational alliances to continue contesting with one another. It allows for modest or far-reaching goals. It even retains traditional glamor, emotional fervor, and heroes. The romance of war continues undimmed into the future.

---

[4] http://www.usfederalbudget.us/defense_budget_2012_3.html

But there are fundamental changes as well. Most immediately and importantly, human beings are not injured or killed, nor are their lands and properties destroyed. Additionally the costs of producing, maintaining, projecting, and implementing the many modern engines of PW destruction are reduced to a small fraction of their current level.

How are these seemingly-incompatible goals achievable? Through a basic reconceptualization of United States war methodology - which, as implemented, will gradually become the model for other war-participants as well. This new type of war is called **MindWar** (MW).

In this book MW is defined and explained. Its goals and tools to achieve those goals are detailed. A practical path to its replacement of PW is outlined. Finally a future planetary environment in which mankind's war-impulse is satisfied by MW is forecast.

What this book cannot do, of course, is to compel the decision for either the United States or any other war-*habitué* to commence the change from PW to MW. And indeed there are powerful interests which would resist such a change, for reasons ranging from war-industrial profiteering to elementary, emotional hatreds of others. Nevertheless, as noted above, the costs for indulging in these PW relics have simply become too great for any nation, and the world collectively, to bear. All that is needed is a practical way out, and MW is that exit and solution.

To whom is this book addressed? It would be nice if all statesmen, politicians, religious- and ideological movement-leaders would read and implement it immediately; but that won't happen. Instead MW needs to be experimentally introduced at a "laboratory" level, both so it can become an example to onlookers, and so that its principles can be refined in practice. Indeed MW is both an art and a science, and neither dimension can be neglected if it is to be successful.

The laboratory proposed in this book is the United States Army, and particularly its "Special Operations Forces (SOF)" component. The reason for this choice will be discussed in the text, as will be its potentialities and limitations.

MindWar went through many drafts prior to publication, and I am deeply grateful to the revered sages who inspired and critiqued its development. Some of these are recognized in the Dedications; others have preferred to remain anonymous. Common to all of them, in my perception and admiration, is the shared conviction that humanity deserves a future and a fate better than self-extermination. [5]

A special appreciation is acknowledged to Dr. Gregory S. Seese, who throughout this project not only critiqued the manuscript but, as an Active senior officer at the John F. Kennedy Special Warfare Center and School, ensured that my impression of its present posture and doctrine was accurate. Dr. Seese, who is branch-qualified not only in Psychological Operations and Civil Affairs but also as a Medical Service Corps officer, personally experienced the reality of PW in Afghanistan and wears the Purple Heart as a permanent reminder of his brush with death.

Additionally I am very grateful to Dr. William Anderson, a distinguished professional in the rare and exclusive field of Neuropsychiatry, for his reflective and incisive Afterword. That MindWar stands up to his

---

[5] In this they stand most dramatically opposed to the infamous Marquis de Sade, who disdained the notion of redemptive philosophy, holding the supreme compulsion of the human race to be its self-destruction; the extinction of the species is therefore not to be regretted, and history is not progress but contemptibly-helpless drifting towards eventual, inescapable annihilation. Cf. Donald Thomas, *The Marquis de Sade* (Boston: New York Graphic Society, 1976).

critical eye is all the more vital given the concept's involvement with not only the psychological but the physical functioning of the human mind.

MindWar would never have completed its mysterious and intricate journey from vision to hypothesis to theory to book without regular sprinklings of greenish-grey pixie-dust by my soul-mate and muse Lilith.

> I expect to pass through this world but once. Any good therefore that I can do, or any kindness that I can show to any fellow creature, let me do it now. Let me not defer or neglect it, for I shall not pass this way again.
>
> - William Penn

As a soldier, a political scientist, and a magician I too shall visit Earth but once, and that briefly. I also am fond of this sublime planet, and thus wish to put forth such learning, experience, and energies as I may uniquely possess in these three fields to enhance its beauty, heal its wounds, and perfect its future. *MindWar* will not be the last word in achieving such goals, but with the inspiration, dedication, and good will of others to build upon it, it may be one of the first.

San Francisco
April 30, 2013

Descende, audas viator, et terrestre centrum attinges. Kod feci.
Descend, audacious traveler, and you will reach the center of the Earth. I did it.

> - Arne Saknussemm
> Jules Verne,
> *Journey to the Center of the Earth,* 1864

Part I: Concept

Chapter 1: MindWar

> **Psychohistory**: That branch of mathematics which deals with the reactions of human conglomerates to fixed social and economic stimuli. Implicit in this definition is the assumption that the human conglomerate being dealt with is sufficiently large for valid statistical treatment. A further necessary assumption is that the human conglomerate be itself unaware of psychohistorical analysis in order that its reactions be truly random.
> - Isaac Asimov, *Foundation*, 1951

> *Áristos* (from the ancient Greek Αριστος): The best for a given situation.
> - John Fowles, *The Áristos*, 1964

A. Antecedent: *MindWar* 1980

In the later 1970s, Psychological Operations (PSYOP) doctrine in the U.S. Army had yet to emerge from the disappointment and frustration of the Vietnam War. Thus it was that in 1980 Colonel Paul Vallely[6], Commander of the 7th PSYOP Group, asked Major Michael Aquino, as his Headquarters PSYOP Research & Analysis (FA) Team Leader, to draft a paper that would

---

[6] Later Major General, USA.

encourage some futurethought within the PSYOP community. He did not want a Vietnam postmortem, but rather some fresh and innovative ideas concerning PSYOP's evolution and application.

I prepared an initial draft, which Vallely reviewed and annotated, which proceeded to revised drafts and critiques until he was satisfied, and the result of that was the concept paper: *From PSYOP to MW: The Psychology of Victory*.[7]

Vallely sent copies of it to various governmental offices, agencies, commands, and publications involved or interested in PSYOP. He intended it not as an article for publication, but simply as a "talking paper" to stimulate dialogue. In this it was quite successful, judging by the extensive and lively letters he received concerning it over the next several months.

Within the U.S. military, PSYOP has habitually been relegated to a back-seat as a "force multiplier". The principal strategic decisions are made in consideration of traditional political and military interests and goals. Only then is PSYOP invited to the table, to help achieve already-agreed-upon missions more efficiently.

Vallely's and my original concept of MW reverses this sequence. Psychological means for achieving victory - essentially through convincing the enemy that he really wants to bring his policies and goals into harmony with ours - are **first** fashioned in support of basic political realities. The use of "ordinary" military force (bombs,

---

[7] The term "MindWar" was coined by another PSYOP officer, Major Richard Sutter, and myself in 1977. After seeing the recent film *Star Wars*, we imagined a play on its name as a futuristic replacement for the bland Army term "Psychological Operations". An avowedly science-fictional treatment of MW, complete with a caricature of Sutter at its helm, appears in my *Star Wars* story *The Dark Side*, 1977 (published in 2016 as *FireForce: A Star Wars Parody*).

bullets, etc.) is regarded as a "last resort" in circumstances wherein MW by itself fails.

The immediate advantage of that 1980 concept of MW is that it conducts wars in nonlethal, noninjurious, and nondestructive ways. Essentially you overwhelm your enemy with argument. You seize control of all of the means by which his government and populace process information to make up their minds, and you adjust it so that those minds are made up as you desire. Everyone is happy, no one gets hurt or killed, and nothing is destroyed.

Ordinary warfare, on the other hand, is characterized by its **rejection** of reason. The antagonists just maim or kill each other's people, and steal or destroy each other's land, until one side is hurt so badly that it gives up [or both sides are hurt so badly that they agree to stop short of victory]. After such a war there is lasting misery, hate, and suffering.

The only losers in MW are the war profiteers: governments, corporations, and entrepreneurs which grow fat on orders for helicopters, tanks, guns, munitions, etc. Consequently what President Dwight Eisenhower referred to as the "military-industrial complex" can be counted upon to resist implementation of MW as the governing strategic conflict doctrine:

> Until the latest of our world conflicts, the United States had no armaments industry. American makers of plowshares could, with time and as required, make swords as well. But we can no longer risk emergency improvisation of national defense. We have been compelled to create a permanent armaments industry of vast proportions. Added to this, three and a half million men and women are directly engaged in the defense establishment. We annually spend on military security alone more than the net income of all United States corporations.
>
> Now this conjunction of an immense military establishment and a large arms industry is new in the American experience. The total influence - economic,

political, even spiritual - is felt in every city, every Statehouse, every office of the Federal government. We recognize the imperative need for this development. Yet, we must not fail to comprehend its grave implications. Our toil, resources, and livelihood are all involved. So is the very structure of our society.

In the councils of government, we must guard against the acquisition of unwarranted influence, whether sought or unsought, by the military-industrial complex. The potential for the disastrous rise of misplaced power exists and will persist. We must never let the weight of this combination endanger our liberties or democratic processes. We should take nothing for granted. Only an alert and knowledgeable citizenry can compel the proper meshing of the huge industrial and military machinery of defense with our peaceful methods and goals, so that security and liberty may prosper together.[8]

As subsequent history evidences, Ike's warning was not heeded, or simply came too late. Indeed the principal, if not exclusive driving force for modern, industrialized nations' wars today is economic advantage and profit, with sociopolitical themes such as "freedom", "democracy", and "national security" merely providing a propaganda veneer to distract and inflame the public. John F. Kennedy's fate after officially deciding to end U.S. military involvement in Vietnam has not been lost on his successors in the White House.[9]

That's the 1980 MW prospectus in its most simplified form.

---

[8] Eisenhower, President Dwight D., Farewell Address, January 17, 1961.

[9] On October 11, 1963 President John F. Kennedy issued [then Top Secret/since declassified] National Security Action Memorandum #263, establishing a 1965 removal of all U.S. military forces from South Vietnam, the first 1,000 to be withdrawn by the end of 1963. Kennedy was assassinated on November 22, 1963. Four days later President Lyndon Johnson issued NSAM #273, reversing #263.

While in the subsequent decade there was no reason to anticipate that this paper would have any official effect upon U.S. PSYOP doctrine within or beyond the Army, several of its prescriptions were applied during the first Gulf War, and recently even more conspicuously during the 2003 invasion of Iraq. In both instances intense PSYOP was directed against the object of the attack, while a simultaneous "Public Affairs" effort was made to shield U.S. domestic public opinion from the type of independent, critical media coverage that plagued the Vietnam War, by "embedding" journalists with military units to inevitably channel their perspectives and perceptions.

The impact of even these minor techniques of MW was remarkable. A psychological climate of inexorable U.S. victory was created and sustained in both the United States and Iraq, which accelerated that outcome on the ground.

Somewhat less positively, the failure of MW in this instance to be guided by only the most rigorous principles of truth and ethics has just as inexorably led to a substantial post-invasion evaporation of that euphoric climate.

Therein lies the Achilles' heel of MW. Invoking as it does the most intense emotions and commitments of its audiences, it **must** deliver the goods **as they are judged by the target audiences**. If the ethical values of those audiences are not respected - if MW is used only in the service of ulterior motives and objectives - the resulting "disintoxication" can be socially shattering.[10]

---

[10] In 1987, consequent to a National War College symposium in which PSYOP was assessed only in terms of expediency, I wrote a research paper for the Industrial College of the Armed Forces, *Psychological Operations: The Ethical Dimension*. Its contentions have been incorporated into this book.

In addition to requiring an absolute ethical anchor, the advanced MW described in this book necessarily extends significantly beyond the time & space boundaries of the immediate battlefield. [In this it differs markedly from Vallely's and my initial concept, which was simply to reverse its battlefield subordination to PW combat.]

B. MindWar Defined

1. Definition

MindWar is the psychological and psychophysiological conditioning of all participants in a sociopolitical problem, first to cooperatively stabilize it without recourse to violence, then to eliminate its basis by the creation of a moral community to supersede it.

Examining the elements of this definition:

- The base term is a composite of:

  - •• the principle of **mind**, which is the collection and correlation of sensory input both actively and passively processed by each self-conscious being in order to draw conclusions, make decision, and take actions accordingly.

  - •• the principle of **war**, which is the extreme expression of intolerance of a current disagreement between at least two social groups when ordinary attempts to resolve it by discussion and diplomacy fail.

- **Psychology** is the study of mind processes and their resultant expression.

- **Psychophysiology** is the branch of psychology which is concerned with the physiological bases of psychological processes.

- **Conditioning** refers to both liminal and subliminal operations of mind modification to produce a desired state of mind perception, interpretation, and behavior. [This problem-tailored mixture of psychological and psychophysiological conditioning is the province of MindWar Branch, and is detailed in Chapter 3.]

- A **sociopolitical problem** is a disagreement between two social and/or political groups of people: nation-states and/or sub- or supra-national cultural, religious, ideological, and/or ethnic groups. War results when the problem is sufficiently persistent and intolerable that it cannot be further endured by the participants.

- **Stabilization** refers to the identification and achievement of the best possible resolution of the problem to temporarily remove the danger of PW: the *áristos*. [This process of stabilization to the *áristos* is the province of MetaForce Branch, and is detailed in Chapter 4.]

- **Nonrecourse to violence** precludes not just PW, but any and all physically harmful measures directed against human beings, whether or not they are problem participants. Such prohibited measures include but are not limited to bodily damage (injury, torture, or murder), exile, imprisonment, and/or destruction of means of livelihood.

- **Creation of a moral community** refers to the process of *ParaPolitics*, resulting not in a structure of exploitation, intimidation, or desperation, but rather in a *polis* based upon enlightened morality: *kalokagathia*. [ParaPolitics and *kalokagathia* are the province of ParaPolitics Branch, and are detailed in Chapter 5.]

2. What It Is

MW controls human external-action thoughts by identifying and adjusting the sensory impressions that the mind uses to assemble, modify, and reinforce them. Humans' sensory-based thoughts form the basis for their constructed outward personalities, and in groups their mores, biases, beliefs, traditions, habits, and taboos. Thus through a graduated process, MW controls groups of humans.

As the size of the group increases, common features of impressions, attitudes, and expressions emerge and can be identified and analyzed statistically, making possible social forecasting and the control of that future by aggregate, not individual manipulation. This is the basis of Isaac Asimov's science-fictional "psychohistory", and of less-ambitious but demonstrably practical Political Science forecasting.[11] Such techniques and procedures can be applied regardless of how such groups are styled or named: cultures, tribes, societies, nations.

Humans usually believe that their individual and collective perceptions and opinions are independently, voluntarily developed. This sense of thought-independence is the basis for the general ideal of the desirability of democracy over other group decision-

---

[11] Cf. Albert Somit, *Political Science and the Study of the Future* (Hinsdale, Illinois: The Dryden Press, 1974).

making systems. A consensus of a majority of independent minds, supposedly, will result in the best and fairest policies for the entire group.

Such a rose-tinted image of democracy is of course an illusion. Both governments and private-sector interests devote intense, constant efforts to shaping public perceptions of reality. From peanut butter to PW, these perceptions are guided subtly, pressed directly, and reinforced socially. By the time the masses are permitted to vote, the parameters of their vote have already been predetermined, with only tokenistic variations in the outcome possible.

Like his PSYOP predecessor, the MWarrior sees behind this curtain of illusion, because professionally he is a weaver of such curtains. This perspective, this clarity of sight, also confronts him with the aforementioned ethical responsibility to exercise his craft according to only the highest and most rigorous values of human individuality and dignity. At any threshold below this, MW would raise the spectre of George Orwell's *1984* Thought Police.

What distinguishes MW from ordinary political/ social/cultural perception- and behavior-influencing efforts is its focus, duration, and intensity. Like PW, MW is a situation-specific operation to deal with a problem of immediate urgency.[12] During this crisis MW overwhelms any existing mundane behavior-dictating systems, replacing them with a more sophisticated, comprehensive, and effective package.

A MW campaign commences when the original destabilizing, pre-PW situation is refashioned into a

---

[12] This is not to imply that MW enters a new situation without prior knowledge of the area and participants in question. Ongoing country/area orientation remains a general responsibility of MWB assets, but a higher level of concentration and asset activation commences once a MW campaign is initiated.

clearly defined and articulated problem (MW Phase 1). The participants are transformed from mutual enemies into allies against that problem as the "common enemy". Phase 1 culminates with a progressively more refined diagnosis of the problem, resulting in formulation of the *áristos* to stabilize it. The process of conditioning and transforming the participants is initiated remotely by MindWar Branch (MWB), and is continued through Phase 4.

In MW Phase 2 the *áristos* is reverse-engineered from accomplishment to the present, to establish the most effective, efficient, and economical path to its realization. The necessary organizations, assets, and bases are devised and assembled.

MW Phase 3 consists of the achievement of the *áristos* under the guidance of MetaForce Branch (MFB) teams, followed by initiation of the permanently corrective moral *polis* by ParaPolitics Branch (PPB) teams.

Phase 4 formalizes MW victory in the completion of the *polis* and departure of PPB. MWB terminates conditioning. The MW campaign structure is then completely dismantled.

3. What It Isn't

a. MW is not "mind control".

The urban-myth image of "government mind-control" is of an insidious, malicious, individuality-destroying technological conspiracy: a sort of "collective lobotomy" to turn the helpless masses into stupefied slaves. [Actually a good case could be made that this is what **PW** attempts to do, which is why it can get people to slaughter one another en masse for no reason.]

The conditioning of MWB has **one and only one purpose**: to change existing, animalistic prejudices and antagonisms into intelligent, amicable cooperation. MWB does not dictate nor even suggest where this cooperation should lead. Once all problem-participants are working together, **they** will go through the steps to identify and establish the *áristos*.

b. MW is not a political ideology.

Old, crude agendæ of "regime change", "democratization", or "anti-[current-bugbearism]" are not part of the MW process. What is important is the achievement of the *áristos*, then a conscientious interest in *kalokagathia*, no matter under what symbolic banner. Some social cultures are accustomed to hierarchical authority since tribal antiquity; others are more comfortable with egalitarianism and diversified political power. MW's interest is simply to remove violence from the equation.

c. MW is not a religion.

Human religions are a consequence of the mystery of the "Why?" of the constitution of the natural universe and the juxtaposition of individual consciousness to it, which MW PSYCONs do not address [and would have no purpose in addressing if they could]. As discussed in Chapter 3.E.2.b, the soul is a manifestation of conceptual consciousness, above and beyond both psychology and psychophysiology. The "morality" of *kalokagathia* is not that of any sectarian religious code or practice, but that of enlightened humanitarianism embracing any natural or supernatural theology.

d. MW is not zombification.

Besides not controlling minds, MW does not destroy them either. Sensationalist media *exposés* of "government-sponsored brain experimentation", whether true or fanciful, have no connection whatever with MW, which is **completely and without exception** non-physically or -medically invasive. Indeed the entire MW campaign process requires that all participants be able and willing to function at their highest level and focus of intelligence, and after Phase 4 the future of the moral *polis* depends upon their self-determined, independent resolve to perpetuate this. [13]

4. The Three Laws of MindWar

Governing all of MW are its three laws:

1. MW is the conduct of war without injury or death to human beings, and without the disruption or destruction of their means of livelihood.

---

[13] For details of zombification see Wade E. Davis , *The Serpent and the Rainbow* (New York: Warner Books, 1987), concerning Haitian Voodoo and actual zombie creation - not by supernatural means, but by the secret use of poisons. The book is based upon field research by the author, who holds undergraduate degrees from Harvard University in Ethnobotany and Biology, and a Ph.D. in Ethnobotany.

Specifically MW-relevant cf. Daniel W. Drezner, *Theories of International Politics and Zombies* (Princeton: Princeton University Press, 2011). Professor Drezner teaches International Politics at Tufts University.

There is no truth whatever to the rumor that the National Security Agency is completely staffed by zombies, though misapprehensions in this regard based upon rare survived encounters are perhaps understandable.

2. While MW includes access to the human mind, this is done only to stimulate its capacity for and interest in cooperative problem-solving.

3. PW is the consequence of MW failure. Therefore MW must not be allowed to fail.

C. Physical War

Is murder a right reserved for that hated nation?
- Captain Nemo, *20,000 Leagues Under the Sea*

In view of the fact that the world is more-or-less constantly at war in multiple locales, and that the term is used frequently in any number of descriptive, argumentative, and emotional contexts, it's surprising how vague its meaning and how few people could define it if asked.

Merriam-Webster's defines "war" (from the 12th-century Anglo/French *werre*) principally as "a state of usually open and declared armed or hostile conflict between states or nations".

Because war is reserved to sovereign states, many acts such as property and territorial theft, demolition, arson, kidnapping, assault, bodily injury, and of course murder, which would be serious crimes if committed by any individual, become legitimized, even praiseworthy. Decorations for "valor" are usually conferred for the mass killing of "the enemy", albeit at risk to oneself. The accidental or incidental killing of innocent bystanders is not "manslaughter" but merely "collateral damage". In the era of strategic bombing, the extermination of entire cities is considered to be legitimate [and "valorous"]. All that is needed to turn these acts from crimes into heroics is for the parent nation to be "at war".

Unsurprisingly no one involved in such acts likes to contemplate this nonsensical distinction. If statesmen and soldiers were forced to apply the same standards and responsibilities to war as to individuals, war would be impossible.

Over the centuries an enormous collection of non-binding idealisms has come into being under the heading of "international law", more recently formalized under various treaties (such as the Geneva Conventions) and multinational organizations (such as the United Nations Charter). These sound civilized and humanitarian, but are enforceable and enforced only to the extent that each warring nation chooses to apply them, which is usually at its convenience. Vanquished nations - as Germany and Japan in World War II - generally find that accountability for "war crimes" is reserved for them, not the victors.

The point of this rather harsh spotlight on the reality of PW is to establish just how cruel and terrible it is, all the more so in the present era of nuclear, biological, and chemical (NBC) weaponry, immensely powerful bombs and other mass-killing devices, and remote/imprecise/impersonal delivery systems. Technologically advanced nations have become adroit at insulating themselves and their citizenry from such distasteful horrors, but they are there - most especially for the unfortunate victims - nevertheless.

As the dictionary reminds us, wars used to be formally declared. This too has become a discarded anachronism since the end of World War II. Partly this has resulted from formal gestures to "outlaw war", such as the Kellogg-Briand Pact of 1928 and Article 2.4 of the United Nations Charter (to both of which the United States is a signatory). PWs, of course, have gone right on - now just relabeled "police actions", "international assistance", or otherwise under the numerous loopholes in the Pact and

Charter. "Only the dead," observed George Santayana, "have seen the end of war."

Moreover when one or more nations resort to PW, neither the rationale for starting it nor the requirements for ending it are anything more than vague exhortations, more to rally domestic support than to communicate principles or standards to the enemy.

> Naturally the common people don't want war. Neither in Russia nor in England nor for that matter in Germany. But after all it is the leaders of the country who determine the policy, and it is always a simple matter to drag the people along, whether it is a democracy or a fascist dictatorship or a parliament or a communist dictatorship. Voice or no voice, the people can always be brought to the bidding of the leaders. That is easy. All you have to do is tell them they are being attacked and denounce the peacemakers for lack of patriotism and exposing the country to danger. It works the same in any country.
> - Reichsmarschall Hermann Göring
>   at the Nürnberg Trials, 1946

Like old soldiers, wars don't end - they just fade away as the combatants tire of the expense, destruction, and human misery, or finally stumble away from them, forgetting what they were supposed to be about in the first place. Journalists and historians rush into justify or condemn them, define their place in history; and as often as not within a few years once-bitter enemies find themselves bedfellows in new, re-enemied alliances. If there is one common thread to all wars, it is that in the long run of human history, they change very little in the course of civilization. They just rough it up along the way.

What is particularly important here is that this haphazard nature of modern PW effectively prevents it from a rationally-planned termination. In other words, if you don't know where it's going or when it's going to get there, you can't reverse-engineer its outcome to the beginning or middle of it. You cannot develop a strategy, a master-plan to make it end quicker, less lethally, or even solving the problem(s) which supposedly made it necessary to begin with.

Nor have history's PWs broken out at necessary, inevitable junctures in antagonists' discourse. They start by impulse or accident, by a grandstanding cannonading of Fort Sumter or a pistol-shot at a visiting Austrian archduke. Sometimes they start for no reason at all, as in the Tonkin Gulf nonincident or Adolf Hitler's memorable speech to the Reichstag that German soldiers "had advanced into Poland and were now defending themselves". The antagonists could have continued trying to resolve their differences civilly and reasonably. They just didn't want to anymore.

> Men love war because it allows them to look serious. Because they imagine that it is the one thing that stops women laughing at them. In it they can reduce women to the status of objects. That is the great distinction between the sexes. Men see objects; women see the relationship between objects. Whether the objects need each other, love each other, match each other. It is an extra dimension of feeling we men are without, and one that makes war abhorrent to all real women - and absurd. I will tell you what war is. War is a psychosis caused by an inability to see relationships. Our relationship with our fellowmen. Our relationship with our economic and historical situation. And above all our relationship to nothingness. To death.
>
> - Maurice Conchis[14]

War is also expensive. It consumes not only human lives [and their potential commercial productivity], but also the materiel necessary to conduct it: weapons, transportation systems, and the entire logistical "tail" these require. Medical costs increase both during combat and long after it has ceased. According to Brown

---

[14] Fowles, John, *The Magus* (Boston: Little, Brown & Company, 1965).

University's online "Costs of War Project", as of April 2015:

> The US federal price tag for the Iraq war - including an estimate for veterans' medical and disability costs into the future - is about $2.2 trillion. The cost for both Iraq and Afghanistan/Pakistan is about $4.4 trillion. Neither of these figures includes future interest costs on borrowing for the wars, which our report estimates at nearly $8 trillion through 2054.[15]

[A trillion is a million million.] By way of comparison, as of 2015 the entire United States public national debt was $18.2 trillion.[16] So in addition to the alternative/constructive purposes for which this PW money could have been spent, its substantial financing costs will continue indefinitely into our future.

"War is not healthy for children and other living things", including those who fight it: What was once called "battle fatigue" and more recently "post-traumatic stress syndrome" has increased in severity to a point where in 2014 the U.S. Army is experiencing more than a soldier-suicide a day.[17]

If modern PW is so destructive, wasteful, and costly, one would think it would be avoided if at all possible. Yet underlying it is not only its appeal to emotional lust [for a simple, satisfying solution to annoyingly-complex problems] but an almost eerie tradition that wars are the definition of nations and their historical legacies.[18]

---

[15] http://watson.brown.edu/costsofwar/

[16] http://www.usgovernmentdebt.us

[17] http://www.stripes.com/news/dod-among-services-army-had-highest-suicide-rate-in-2014-1.393144

[18] Are wars anything but the means whereby a nation is nourished, whereby it is strengthened, whereby it is buttressed? - The Marquis de Sade

What we must conclude of war, therefore, is that, though irrational and nonsensical, it is nevertheless both emotionally desirable and socially inevitable. It cannot be stopped. It can, however, be transformed.

D. MindWar Transformation

MW is not a solution for every conflict that may arise. Nor, if it is implemented, will it necessarily be either a complete or a permanent solution. What it is is a preferred alternative to PW, an *áristos*, which should be tried first. If it is successful, so much the better for everyone concerned. If it fails, the participants retain the option to fall back on PW. Indeed, as discussed above, it is the undesirable alternative of PW that gives MW its principal "weapon". It is in everyone's interest that it **not** fail.

It is the goal of MW to, while fulfilling man's need for war, rechannel its expression into positive, orderly, and nondestructive procedures. To see how this is possible, we will take a closer look at its four [minus 1] phases:

1. Phase Ø: Cessation of Proxy or Covert PhysWar[19]

In an era when the conduct of undeclared war, often through intelligence agency paramilitary forces, mercenaries, proxy nations, and "military advice/aid", has become the norm, all such devices for PW actions must be discontinued. If they are allowed during the prewar/ diplomacy period of relations between the parties, they will:

---

[19] For a detailed discussion of Phase 0, see Chapter 6.

a. Exacerbate immediate and lasting emotional hatred between the parties.

b. Because of their covert, devious, unacknowledged nature, destroy any atmosphere of trust between the parties.

c. Generate death, injury, and damage to both parties which will proportionately increase the difficulty of reaching a mutually-acceptable solution for both.

d. Cause onlooking third nations/groups/ individuals to view any subsequent MW actions with cynicism, as being mere superficial formality in a conflict which has already escalated past that point of resolution.

2. Phase 1: The Redefinition of an Assigned Conflict in Terms of an Acceptable and Practical Outcome.[20]

PW is characterized by a progressively-deteriorating diplomatic situation in which one or more parties eventually lose patience, are overcome by fear or anger, or are emotionally moved by dramatic incident from reason into violence.

In the case of the United States, this country has a strong tradition of civilian control of foreign policy and the diplomatic process generally. DOD is not invited into a situation until the gauntlet has been thrown down, whereupon it is expected not to retrieve it but to simply commence PW. No goal, no measure of victory [in these euphemistic days "exit strategy"] accompanies such an order to march. Vaguely it is assumed that such niceties will come later, after - in the traditionally-meaningless

---

[20] For a detailed discussion of Phase 1, see Chapter 7.

jargon, "the situation has been developed". PW being a progressive and random application of blunt-instrument destruction by all combatants, however, such actual goals and requirements for its cessation never do appear. The vagaries simply continue until pressures unrelated to the actual PW contest bring it to a clumsy, unproductive fade-out.

a. Declaration of MindWar

The first reform of MW, therefore, is one of **demarcation**. It begins with a formal declaration of MW and ends with an equally formal declaration of peace. Before these are brushed aside as archaic ceremonies, consider the reasons for them. The purposes of a declaration of MW are:

(1) to require the Congress to meet its responsibility under the Constitution Article I.8.11 to decide when the United States takes any international or supranational conflict from diplomacy to war. Such a decision, which directly affects countless lives on all sides, is simply too consequential to be abandoned to the current President - who, of course, is himself not an independent decision-maker in such matters even if personally well-intentioned.

The rationale for Article I.8.11 was not just to ensure that the United States would not be rashly dragged or tricked into war. It was also to ensure that, if a war were declared by the elected representatives of the national citizenry, a proportionate number of that citizenry would understand and agree with the vote. In short, when the United States declares war, the entire country should be behind it. It should never be a *fiat* by a clique which the people neither understand nor endorse. That is the formula to **lose** a war from the moment it is begun, as we have experienced all too often in our post-World War II series of *fiat* wars.

(2) to state clearly the circumstances which have caused further diplomacy to be rejected in favor of war.

This is an explanation for three audiences: the citizenry of the United States, the opponent country or group, and the onlooking rest of the world. Each must be convinced that the stated reasons are both complete and sincere. Otherwise:

(a) the U.S. citizenry will suspect that it has been deceived, and will not support the war.

(b) the opponent will not accurately understand why it is being attacked, which prevents it from knowledgeably trying to address those reasons if it wishes to do so, and also immediately antagonizes it with the suspicion that the attack is for ulterior, more venial reasons.

(c) the rest of the world will not see the justice of the U.S. attack, and may assume that it is mere predatory aggression. This is not just a public-relations consideration, as third parties are often drawn into ongoing wars as they spread and escalate. The sooner and more definitively that the United States can establish its just cause, the less chance it will be surprised by overt or covert additional enemies later on.

(3) to state equally clearly the goal of the war, e.g. the conditions for its conclusion.

Without such a statement, neither side knows where it's going or what it's doing. The war becomes a stumble-around in a darkened room, with plenty of tripping over furniture and running into walls, and no open doors with illuminated exit-signs.

If, on the other hand, the United States makes it clear what it requires to stop the war, this country can direct its efforts, including popular support, towards achieving that goal. The enemy country also knows what the United States wants of it, and can immediately or subsequently decide whether to comply. Onlooking third parties can more clearly estimate whether the war might or should involve them, or whether they can effectively steer clear of it.

b. Diagnosis of the "Disease"

PW treats the **symptoms** of the disease only; MW treats the **causes** of the disease.

As part of the Declaration process, the root problem or problems of the destabilizing situation must be clearly and objectively identified in terms of both policies/ systems and those individuals or groups controlling them. In many ways this will be the most difficult and exacting requirement of the MW process, because it calls for cold, unrationalizing honesty in all directions. There must be no off-the-table "sacred cows": no traditional or habitual assumptions favoring either party's desires that can pre-skew and potentially derail a MW solution. Among such "sacred cows" [for **both** parties]:

(1) The acquisition or possession of nuclear or any other advanced form of weaponry.

(2) Creation or preservation of economic advantage, either for a centralized economy or national industrial/trade interests.[21]

(3) Type of government, whether autocratic, oligarchic, democratic, theocratic, or any variation on these.

(4) Internal national policies, customs, or issues bearing indirectly upon the conflict.

(5) The demands or desires of uninvolved third parties, whether other nations seeking to profit from the situation, supranational religious institutions, or international bodies such as the United Nations or NATO.

c. Prescription of the "Cure": The *Áristos*

The moment there is a formal Declaration of MindWar, all "sacred cows" become secondary to the primary task, which is MW victory. If and when that is accomplished and the Defense Department returns the situation to civilian institutions, the "pasture" is once again their concern.

Irrelevant and unessential considerations ("sacred cows") discarded, the key elements causing the situation are identified. These will be unique to each situation, of course, so cannot be forced into standardized definitions or habitual responses to them.

In the case of a territorial dispute, for instance, the disputing parties must be identified. It may be international, or intertribal, or religious factional,

---

[21] There are powerful emotional and economic interest groups in favor of PW, who can be counted upon to resist its replacement by MW generally.

political ideological, or a mixture of more than one of these. In each situation we know only that the United States is one of the parties.

The situation is then analyzed in terms of:

(1) Its desired solution for each party.

(2) The most beneficial solution for each party (which may not be identical to the desired one).

(3) The minimum effective solution for each party.

(4) The minimum tolerable solution for each party (which may not be identical to the minimum effective one).

These solutions are next plotted in a matrix within an overall time- and cost-boundary, and the intersections examined for matches. Ideally a match will appear to fit (1) or (2) intersections, but probably not. So the MWarrior examines all (3) and (4) intersections, looking for the simplest, quickest, most economical, and least PW-triggering intersection. This becomes the MW victory objective, which the United States then openly announces to all parties.

All participants are now aware of the U.S. Declaration of MW, the reasons for it, and the *áristos* for its conclusion.

We now enter the difficult area of "civilian control of the military". It is an old complaint of the U.S. Military that its civilian superiors meddle in its conduct of an assigned war, screwing it up. Civilians respond with the mantra that "war is too important to be left to generals" and that [as indeed in PW] the blind application of brute force solves nothing.[22]

MW must therefore at this point start the continuous process of presenting its case to its civilian superiors.

3. Phase 2: The reverse-engineering of the decided outcome from its establishment back to the present situation.[23]

The purpose of this is simply to identify all of the component changes that will be necessary to accomplish the desired transformation. If one or more components are found to be impossible, then the overall goal needs to be reconceptualized or reduced until it is practically achievable.

Here sociopolitical and economic forecasting techniques are essential. Present policy options must be extended and extrapolated. The aggregate of these must be analyzed into a cross-matrix to ascertain whether there are any incompatibilities. Any developing component-change must be reentered into the matrix to ensure that the totality remains viable.

From each completed matrix a MW map emerges: "how to get there from here". As with Phase 1, this map must be understandable by and acceptable to United States decision-makers at all levels. A MW matrix must stand on all of its feet to be effective, and if any one of them is undermined, the matrix collapses.

Thus the consensus arrived at in Phase 1 must survive Phase 2, which means that the general and ideal must survive its translation into the specific and practical.

---

[22] Everybody wants ta get inta de act. - Jimmy Durante

[23] For a detailed discussion of Phase 2, see Chapter 8.

4. Phase 3: MW Attack.[24]

The matrix is set in motion. Its components are assigned to appropriate implementation units, and those units delegate them further down to implementation action elements.

A simultaneous, continuous feedback system is instituted so that every action, inaction, success, and failure is fed back into the overall MW matrix. If a failure is examined and found to be correctible, the action is retried until successful. If it is evaluated as uncorrectable, and cannot be compensated for at higher-intermediate levels, the MW matrix is again adjusted to reduce the overall goal accordingly.

This process of feedback and matrix goal-reduction is not to be understood as an "easy-out". MW is just that: a war. It is a deliberate effort to change the enemy. This is rarely a simple or easy task. MW requires outthinking the enemy at all times and stages of the conflict, and this is a constant, demanding process. The MW matrix is no good if it is reduced to zero, or to a fiction of actual accomplishment. It must be pressed forward, forced into existence by the full will and skill of the United States. Only where it is discovered to be intrinsically flawed should it be modified.

5. Phase 4: MindWar Victory[25]

Once the MW matrix is achieved, formal victory is declared and the war is immediately and absolutely ended. This is a signal to the vanquished enemy that it is no longer under attack, and to the United States

---

[24] For a detailed discussion of Phase 3, see Chapter 9.

[25] For a detailed discussion of Phase 4, see Chapter 10.

government and citizenry that no more assets are to be so devoted.

The formal, unilateral declaration of peace is just as important to the concept of MW as the earlier declaration of war. Current PW eliminates both, with the result that not only is the Constitution ignored but the nation and the world not given a clear and unequivocal signal of both:

- With the declaration of war, all responsibility is turned over to the Defense Department. Exterior activity, such as by the Intelligence community, ceases. This so as not to interfere with the MW matrix.

- With the declaration of peace, both the United States and the vanquished country know that the MW campaign is finally and fully halted. International relations are returned to normal diplomatic and commercial venues. The Intelligence community can now be reengaged if appropriate. [Cf. Chapter 3 concerning the role of intelligence in MW.]

That's it.

Upon a first reading, one may be taken aback by the apparent simplicity of this Phase-structure. This is not only intentional but indeed essential. Recourse to the current U.S. Army MISO[26]   manuals quickly induces MEGO[27]; over the years PSYOP has become the darling of innumerable staff studies, think tanks, and cartons of eggheads. The result is something that no one can actually use.

---

[26] "Military Information Support Operations": since 2010, the humorously transparent effort to disguise PSYOP with a soothing euphemism. Occasionally confused with a Japanese soup, and immortalized by a famous line in Stanley Kubrick's 1987 film *Full Metal Jacket*.

[27] MEGO: My Eyes Glaze Over [from reading material that is too long, too complex, and too incomprehensible].

The concept and component phases of MW must be simple, easy-to-use, flexible, and intuitive. Its focus can be broadened and extended at progressively-higher echelons, but the techniques themselves must be as simple to use as a Boy Scout pocketknife. Only thus will MW be able to react instantly to changing conditions, and to remain two steps ahead of the enemy.

In Part II each of the MW branches and their functions are examined in detail. Then in Part III the five Phases of a MW campaign are discussed, to include the mixture of branch expertise necessary for their success.

Part II: Army War Branches

Chapter 2: The PhysWar Branches

What is the spirit of the bayonet? **TO KILL!**
- U.S. Army Infantry School

A. The PhysWar Mission of the Army

The Army's mission is to fight and win our Nation's wars by providing prompt, sustained land dominance across the full range of military operations and spectrum of conflict in support of combatant commanders. We do this by:
• Executing Title 10 and Title 32 United States Code directives, to include organizing, equipping, and training forces for the conduct of prompt and sustained combat operations on land.
• Accomplishing missions assigned by the President, Secretary of Defense and combatant commanders, and Transforming for the future.[28]

So states the U.S. Army's official website. What this means in practice is that the Army is designed and organized for PW through its backbone Combat Arms branches: Infantry, Armor/Cavalry, and Field/Air Defense Artillery. Often grouped with these are Aviation, the [combat] Corps of Engineers and the Signal Corps; and behind these are numerous "combat support" and "combat service support" branches. In principle and practice, they all exist to maximize the Army's PW combat power, which is to kill, capture, and/or destroy

---

[28] http://www.army.mil/info/organization/

whatever is defined as "the enemy" by higher authority (in practice the President and in theory the Congress of the United States).

The other armed services - the Air Force, Navy, and Marine Corps - have similar general mission statements reflecting their operational environments. But it is the Army which focuses predominantly upon land operations, and land is where people live and their means of livelihood are established. As the Army is configured and employed, so necessarily must follow the other services.

B. "Special Operations" Branches in the PhysWar Army

In addition to the traditional/established combat branches of the Army, there presently exist three "Special Operations" branches which, until the implementation of MW, function simply to augment, support, and clean up after PW campaigns.[29] Thus they are in effect, if not in self-image, "battlefield janitors".

The oldest of these, Civil Affairs Branch, was formally established in 1955 as the Civil Affairs & Military Government Branch, USAR, following a long history of less-formal, events-driven offices and organizations within the Army to deal with post-PW civilian crises. In 1961 it was expanded into an Active Army branch as well, though it remains accessible by post-commissioning [officer] transfer only.

The other two branches - Special Forces and Psychological Operations - came into being as "branch immaterial" specialties following World War II. Thus officers course-qualified for them retained their original

---

[29] This book considers the recently-created Electronic Warfare Branch as a combat support branch similar to the Signal Corps, rather than a component of Special Operations.

branch affiliations, and normally returned to them after temporary assignments to SF/PSYOP units. Special Forces was finally formalized as a branch in 1987, and Psychological Operations 2006.

As reviewed in Chapters #3-5, CA, SF, and PSYOP shared not only their "battlefield janitor" status, but a distinctly non-destructive doctrinal orientation. CA was expected to rebuild destroyed population infrastructures; SF was to teach and train local military & paramilitary individuals & groups; and PSYOP was to attempt to control both civil & military audiences through propaganda.

In the new MW environment, the relationship of these three branches to the PW branches of the Army is conceptually reversed. The "Special Operations" branches - now evolved into new designs, functions, and names - become the Army's **initial and principal** means of fulfilling its mission. The PW branches and their support systems become a less-desirable alternative to be employed only if MW fails. Indeed it is their very undesirability - the prospect of the death, injury, and destruction they inflict - that encourages all the more interest in a MW solution by all involved groups and individuals.

C. The MindWar Mission of the Army

Since its creation on 14 June 1775, the U.S. Army has been an institution and an engine of death and destruction, albeit and avowedly to preserve and protect the United States and its citizenry. MindWar proposes to change the Army's operational methodology to a completely constructive and creative one, with its PW power maintained and brandished as the same sort of unthinkable deterrent as the nation's nuclear arsenal. Thus other nation-states and nonstate groups will have no alternative but to choose the MW option, which, once they do, they will discover works entirely to their rescue and regeneration.

The evolution to MindWar will be complete when the arrival of any U.S. Army soldier, indeed any U.S. servicemember, anywhere in the world is looked upon by everyone present as a blessing.

Chapter 3: MindWar Branch[30]
[Formerly:
Psychological Operations Branch]

It's kind of fun to do the impossible.
- Walt Disney

------

[30] The MindWar Branch (MWB) insignia replaces the old PSYOP Branch:

The crossed daggers, whose blades are in the Branch colors of Negative Green and Cerebral Grey, glow from hilt to tip, signifying MW's radiant power, and end in lightning bolts symbolic of MW's control of the electromagnetic spectrum. The chesspiece knight is portrayed as a swirling ghost, representing the hidden yet dynamic nature of MW. Its image alternates between complete existence (black) and nonexistence (clear), conveying not only its illusionary presence but the chess knight's ability to move and strike mysteriously. The horse's eye is red, as he is a horse of war. The base of the chesspiece is struck with the Greek letters *psi* (the powers of the mind) and *phi* (the universal symbol of perfection/the "Golden Ratio"). Thus combined they convey the power of the human consciousness raised to perfection. MWB unit members wear the grey beret with all uniforms except the dress blue.

A. The Old Concepts

1. Psychological Operations

Psychological Operations (PSYOP[31]) is an often-misunderstood term, and both it and its specialized aspects will bear clarification prior to the discussion of its role in the American military culture and its evolution into MindWar. From the U.S. Army's final[32] PSYOP manual:

> **Psychological Operations (PSYOP)**: Planned operations to convey selected information and indicators to foreign audiences to influence their emotions, motives, objective reasoning, and ultimately the behavior of foreign governments, organizations, groups, and individuals. The purpose of Psychological Operations is to induce or reinforce foreign attitudes and behavior favorable to the originator's objectives.[33]

2. Psychological Warfare

The related and more traditional term "Psychological Warfare" had been retired to the Orwellian memory hole by 2007, but previously:

> **Psychological warfare (PSYWAR)** is the planned use of propaganda and other psychological actions to influence the opinions, emotions, attitudes, and behavior of hostile foreign groups in such a way as to support the achievement of national objectives.[34]

---

[31] **Not** "PSYOPS" or "Psy Ops"!

[32] Before sanitizing its Field Manual titles to "MISO" in 2012.

[33] FM 3-05.301, *Psychological Operations Process: Tactics, Techniques, and Procedures*, 30 August 2007, Glossary-8.

[34] FM 33-1: *Psychological Operations*. Washington, D.C.: Department of the Army, 31 August 1979, page #H-3.

Note that in these definitions *per se* there is no mention of "the truth" or of the United States' commitment to it. They are simply "mission-oriented" definitions. To be sure, they could be phrased thus to encompass the PSYOP and PSYWAR of all nations, not just the United States. The implication of their definition thus in U.S. PSYOP manuals, however, is that this **is** the way **we** look at them.

3. Propaganda

The stock-in-trade of pre-MW PSYOP was **propaganda**, which is:

> ... any form of communication in support of national objectives designed to influence the opinions, emotions, attitudes, or behavior of any group in order to benefit the sponsor, either directly or indirectly.[35]

Despite exhaustive efforts to "respectabilize" it, propaganda as a concept still labors under the negative image Joseph Goebbels and his Propaganda Ministry created during the Third Reich. Goebbels' passion for the utility of propaganda led him to an arrogant contempt for uncontrolled, purposeless information. In his eyes the motivational and indoctrinational goals of the German propaganda effort fully justified the complete selection and packaging of information as might be convenient or expedient:

> Success is the important thing. Propaganda is not a matter for average minds, but rather a matter for

---

[35] *Ibid.* FM 3-05.301, *op. cit.*, page #Glossary-8. the MISO-generation manual, FM 3-53, January 2013, continues this "Army" definition but notes that the Joint Service definition (JP 3-13.2) now restricts "propaganda" to "adversary communication, especially of a biased or misleading nature" (page #Glossary-10).

practitioners. It is not supposed to be lovely or theoretically correct. I do not care if I give wonderful, æsthetically elegant speeches, or speak so that women cry. The point of a political speech is to persuade people of what we think right. I speak differently in the provinces than I do in Berlin, and when I speak in Bayreuth, I say different things than I say in the Pharus Hall. That is a matter of practice, not of theory. We do not want to be a movement of a few straw brains, but rather a movement that can conquer the broad masses. Propaganda should be popular, not intellectually pleasing. It is not the task of propaganda to discover intellectual truths.

It is thus not surprising that today, in most people's eyes, "propaganda" has simply become a synonym for utilitarian unconcern with the truth. [36]

In the above-cited American definition, the standard by which propaganda is measured is a mission-oriented one, in which "national interest" is the determining factor. Once more this definition can be excused as applicable to all propaganda, not just that of the United States; but in that case the door is again left open for the U.S. to utilize propaganda per that same rationale. At least up to 1979 [but, curiously, absent from all subsequent manuals] the Army made the following statement concerning its propaganda:

> U.S. Army propaganda is based on a strategy of truth. It seeks to strengthen or create a favorable image by emphasizing the credible truth. This is so because the complete truth is frequently not believable by the target audience.
>
> Dedication to the truth does not imply that a full recounting of facts is required or advisable. Facts to support certain themes may be selected while others may be

---

[36] "The United States has no propaganda to peddle, since we are neither advocates nor defenders of any dogma so fragile or doctrine so frightened as to require it." - President Lyndon B. Johnson, at the swearing-in of USIA Director Leonard Marks, September 1965.

excluded. The propagandist reports those facts that present his side in the best light ...[37]

What differentiates a "**strategy** of truth" from just "**the** truth"? Is the truth uttered merely because it is thought to be less vulnerable than lies, or because of a commitment to it that is above and beyond motives of advantage or expedience? And is the selective presentation of facts [and exclusion of others bearing upon the situation] justifiably considered "the truth" - even if done to enhance the "credibility" of a message to an audience?[38]

In traditional "battlefield janitor" MISO, propaganda frequently takes the form of simple, crude messages directed at low-level PW combatants, coaxing them to retreat, defect, or revolt. The motivations invoked are similarly basic: fear, greed, comfort, personal safety, vengeance. Its effectiveness is directly proportionate to battlefield conditions: victorious soldiers will ignore it, while defeated ones will clutch at it. Either way it is recognized as something inherently insulting and shameful to the recipient - an image which reflects back upon its ostensible source: the United States.

Dissemination of crude propaganda also undermines the effectiveness of any higher-echelon actions targeting leadership, simply by springing from the same source. If the United States is perceived to be cynical and contemptuous on one level, it will be seen through this lens on all levels.

---

[37] FM 33-1, *op.cit.*, page # 11-7.

[38] "Credibility and truth do not necessarily march in step in psychological warfare. What is said, written, printed or broadcasted in the field must be credible within the terms in which it is projected; it need not necessarily be the truth in every instance. In fact the truth can in certain circumstances defeat credibility." - Charles Roetter, *Psychological Warfare* (London: B.T. Batsford Ltd, 1974).

Propaganda's effectiveness is inversely proportional to the degree of belief and behavior modification it proposes. To understand this, the propagandist must realize that people do not "change their minds"; rather they reinterpret and reevaluate their existing thought-patterns of reality as they are so motivated.

4. The Shades

Confusion over the terms "white", "grey", and "black" propaganda is common, so it may be helpful to review their definition as well before proceeding further. Note that all three shades of propaganda are **source**-determined. The color-coding does **not** refer to the truthfulness of the propaganda message **itself**:

> **White propaganda** is propaganda in which the source is openly and accurately stated.
> **Grey propaganda** is propaganda in which no source is stated.
> **Black propaganda** is propaganda in which the source is deliberately and explicitly misrepresented.[39]

5. General Parameters

What is evident in the above definitions is that PSYOP as a tool is generally understood to be **mission-justified**, and further that its potential use includes **deliberate falsehood**.

These features do not in themselves invalidate PSYOP as a U.S. policy option, any more than a rifle's potential for unethical use invalidates its place as a tool in support

---

[39] *Ibid.*, page #11-2. In 2011 the Joint Chiefs of Staff officially replaced the traditional "Black/Grey/White" terms with "concurring or organizational attribution/delayed attribution/nonattribution", ostensibly for further PSYOP image MISO-sanitizing. (CJCSI 3110.05E, 30 September 2011). This book uses the traditional terminology.

of ethical ends. What **is** important is that, like the rifle, PSYOP can be used unethically just as easily as it can be used ethically. The mere fact that it is the United States who employs it does **not in itself** validate it from an ethical standpoint.

6. Beyond Propaganda: The Influence Continuum

The rationale for propaganda is that if a believable message is delivered to an audience, that audience will modify its behavior accordingly. This is based on two assumptions: that people construct their beliefs and attitudes by reason, and that they can be further inspired to act in furtherance of them by reason.

As examined below under "E. Thought Architecture", this is a fatally-flawed misapprehension. 95% of human thinking is subconscious, and further takes the form of response to accustomed patterns. Only the remaining 5% is conscious, and only part of that is the consequence of reason (e.g. algorithmic).

In his current examination of the science of PSYOP, Dr. Gregory Seese rejects the usefulness of propaganda entirely; indeed the "P-word" is not mentioned even once therein.[40] Within the realm of conscious/reasoned thought, Seese identifies a five-stage "influence continuum", from the least to the most forceful: (1) Information & Education, (2) Persuasion, (3) Compliance, (4) Coercion, and (5) Thought Reform. In PSYOP campaigns the first four of these may be employed both independently and concertedly as the situation demands them, with their effectiveness

---

[40] Major Gregory S. Seese, Psy.D., *The Science of Influence: A Primer for Psychological Operations* (v3.3), 2013).

measured strictly by any consequent change in target audience **behavior**.

Level 5 (Thought Reform) is the Continuum's theoretical extreme, but because of the intense psychological pressure involved must **not** be used by the United States. It is perhaps best exemplified by the "brainwashing" torture notorious during the capitalist/communist Cold War, and thus results more in severe mental damage than in any useful or productive behavioral modification.

Level 4 (Coercion) is also MW-prohibited, since it is a somewhat imprecise level extending from "PSYOP of the deed" [as in compel people to safety when they are faced with battlefield danger] to the MW-unacceptable extremes of physical threats or harm to force obedience.

Thus mere changing of beliefs or opinions, as attempted for instance in surveys or interrogations, is inadequate. What is material and relevant is action, specifically action commenced and changed in cooperation with the campaign objectives.

The crude instrument of propaganda has no place in this continuum; at none of its levels is there distortion, omission, or falsification of information concerning the message. The graduated emphasis is dictated more by available-time and -resource constraints: In a PW battlefield environment, for instance, there is obviously little time for leisurely education and more of an urgency for essentially-succinct instructions.

Within the universe of MW, Seese's continuum pertains to Liminal Involuntary Psycontrol (LIPC).[41] In this area it is the most comprehensive formula for obtaining behavioral results, and in situations of extreme urgency and pressure quite probably the most practical

---

[41] See E.3 below.

and productive. The subliminal realms (SLIPC) generally require much more time, precision, and intricacy.

B. Key Principles of the American Military Culture

PSYOP's place within the Army is a function of the generally-accepted values of that institution, which in turn represent what the Army perceives as its proper posture within the culture of the United States generally. Key principles of the American military culture include:

1. Primacy of the Constitution

The existence and actions of the military are held to be justified by [and in defense of] the United States Constitution. It is significant that the oath of an American serviceman is to **this** document, **not** to a particular individual, office, government, or administration. The effect of this orientation is to place the military at least theoretically within an "ethical universe" that is more or less purely Lockean.

John Locke (1632-1704)   was responsible for the doctrine that all government should be limited in its powers and exists only by consent of the governed. He introduced the concepts of "inalienable rights" (which cannot be contracted away to the government or anyone else) and that "all men are created equal".

Locke based his political philosophy upon reason, paying lip service to rational ideals. He wanted to build a system that would reflect "basic man" rather than one which sets ideals and expectations for him that he cannot reach. The advantage of this kind of system is that it never overreaches itself and rarely falls victim to hypocrisy of a structural sort, since not much except cooperation and stability is expected of it. The disadvantage is that it is a difficult system to improve by inspired or intellectual leadership, since political power is concentrated in majority opinion - which tends to be sluggish, conservative, complacent, and apathetic - unless a crisis shocks it into action. Political power can be corrupted through the economic, social, or demagogic manipulation of the people.

The "self-evident truths" in this perceptual universe are accepted as articles of faith which need no argumentative justification.

Indeed to question the assumptions underlying the Constitution would be viewed as a kind of quasi-religious heresy - as indeed it is from a philosophical perspective. The social-contract theorists of the Enlightenment held a vague, general disbelief that God, if he were presumed to exist, would disregard the operation of natural laws to take an interest in the behavior of individual human beings for better or worse. Generally termed *Deism*, this belief-system included such Founding Fathers as George Washington, Benjamin Franklin, Thomas Jefferson, James Madison, Alexander Hamilton, and Thomas Paine. They therefore designed ideal governmental systems in which human reason was preeminent, with traditional Judæo/Christian divine influence being relegated to a ceremonial and symbolic role in actual political decision-making.

2. Individual Ethics

Ethics, alternatively called **moral philosophy**, seeks to distinguish what is good from what is bad and to formulate justifiable reasons for making such distinctions. **Philosophy** generally refers to the rational examination of an individual's or group's core principles.

As a branch of philosophy, ethics is a **normative** science; that is, it seeks to identify principles of good and evil that transcend social, cultural, or political convention (social contract theory).

Beyond a merely normative approach to ethics is **metaethics**, which seeks to investigate normative currency-terms such as "good", "evil", "justice", "ought", "right", and "wrong". The neutrality and objectivity of metaethics presume that such terms are not dependent upon moral beliefs (such as religion). The metaethical concept of **naturalism**, advanced by theorists such as John Dewey and Herbert Spencer, posits that moral terms have a basis in scientific fact. **Intuitionists** agree that moral terms have an external, reliable basis but attribute it to self-evident ("I know it when I see it") qualities.

Challenging intuitionists and naturalists are **moral skepticists** who insist that moral terms are completely arbitrary. **Emotivists** claim that such terms have no capacity for being true or false in themselves, and that the people who use them are simply stating their emotions about an issue. **Subjectivists** maintain that moral judgments state subjective facts only about attitudes, not the objects of those attitudes. And **Imperativists** insist that moral judgments are actually "commands" in another guise, hence do not focus at all on criteria of truth or objectivity.

When even its basic language terms are so fraught with controversy, normative ethics is off to a rough start. Beyond this are arguments over the criteria for making **any** kind of moral judgment. **Teleologists** maintain that the morality of an action is determined solely by its consequences. Some teleologists, such as Plato, insist that the perfection of the self is the correct consequence; hedonists say that it is mere pleasure; utilitarians counter that it must be the greatest benefit to society. **Theologians**, such as Aquinas, Luther, *et al.*, dispense with teleology altogether in favor of obedience to proclaimed or perceived morality from a God or gods.

The sharpest attack on ethics generally comes from **egoists** such as Thomas Hobbes and Friedrich Nietzsche (*cf.* his *Genealogy of Morals*), who consider all ethics as verbal camouflage to conceal the reality that all actions are merely in the interest of the stronger (who by that same strength dictate all definitions of "justice", "right", etc.). The egoist position was represented in the Platonic Dialogue *The Republic* by Glaucon, and went on to form the basis for Enlightenment "social contract" theories (Hobbes, Locke, Rousseau), wherein "justice" and related terms became just matters of agreement and contract between the people of a society.

Accordingly it is not surprising that practical problem-solvers shy away from metaethical issues and try rather to address questions in terms of what are generally called **descriptive ethics** - the customs and standards of a given culture which serve as measurements of rightness and wrongness within that culture. An acceptance of descriptive ethics as ethics leads to an attitude of **ethical relativism**, according to which there is no standard for judging right and wrong apart from the cultural environment of specific situations. Hence the killing of humans by humans may be "ethical" if sanctioned by a judge or national sovereign, but the identical act may be "unethical" if undertaken by an individual, regardless of reasons.

Until the Enlightenment of the late-17th and 18th centuries, ethical philosophy was completely metaethical; standards of good and evil were accepted as being prescribed by one or more divinities or divine principles (Egyptian *neteru*, Platonic Forms). It was humanity's task not to determine ethics, but rather to understand and obey divinely-ordained ethics.

Inherent in the American military culture, at least theoretically, is the responsibility of each individual for his own ethical behavior - and for the issuance of ethical commands to subordinates. Although the oath of military service also stipulates obedience to superior authority, this is theoretically subordinate to one's personal ethical responsibility and cannot be used to excuse unethical acts. This, of course, was raised to the level of explicit doctrine as a consequence of the post-World War II Nürnberg trials, in which German officials had unsuccessfully argued that their oaths of obedience to Adolf Hitler superseded, hence excused actions on their part which outraged prevailing Western norms.

The word "theoretically" appears twice in the above paragraph for a deliberate reason. Although the so-called "Nürnberg Principle" is officially accepted by the United States, it is a difficult standard to apply [or enforce] in practice.

The reason for this difficulty ought now to be clear: It requires individuals to make decisions according to ethical criteria which they do not understand save as vague articles of faith. The best that can be hoped for is a Stoic reliance upon impressions of situations to be reliable ones.

Stoicism was a philosophical system holding that it is man's duty to freely conform to natural law and his destiny, that virtue is the highest good, and that the wise man should be free from passion, equally unperturbed by joy or grief. First introduced by Zeno, a somewhat mysterious Phœnician/Egyptian (336-264 BCE), it was later espoused by Chrysippus, Cicero, Seneca, Epictetus, and Emperor Marcus Aurelius of Rome.

In the "social contract" atmosphere of the Enlightenment [and American Revolution], judgment of such situational impressions was generally taken to be based upon what the philosopher David Hume

(1711-1776) described as "prevailing passionate custom". According to this standard, reason may be used to discover the "fitting" - the most practical or sensible approach - but not the "morally good". Hence virtue and vice are products of sentiment. Virtue is not approved because it is virtue; it is considered to be virtue because it meets with passionate approval.

Even with such conventionalized guidelines, it is difficult for a soldier, particularly of junior rank and/or limited education, to venture an ethical judgment overruling that of a senior. There is always the excuse that the senior is presumed to be aware of [and have taken into consideration] aspects of the situation of which the junior is ignorant.

3. *Law of* [PW] *War*

The United States has devoted an extensive and exhaustive publication - the *Law of War Manual*, published 2015 by the Department of Defense General Counsel - in support of PW ethics.

Unfortunately the same *Manual* blanket-exempts the United States from compliance with it, reducing it to a mere propaganda exercise:

> This manual represents the legal views of the Department of Defense. This manual does not, however, preclude the Department from subsequently changing its interpretation of the law.
>
> Although the preparation of this manual has benefited from the participation of lawyers from the Department of State and the Department of Justice, this manual does not necessarily reflect the views of any other department or agency of the U.S. Government or the views of the U.S. Government as a whole.
>
> This manual is not intended to, and does not, create any right or benefit, substantive or procedural, enforceable at law or in equity against the United States, its departments,

agencies, or other entities, its officers or employees, or any other person.[42]

4. Worth of the Individual

As the individual is placed at the center of the Lockean universe, being in effect a "sacred object", each individual's ethics are an essential personal responsibility. In certain other cultures the individual is considered to be a mere component of the state, or of a class, or of an ethnic group. In such cases the right and responsibility to determine and judge ethics is similarly removed.

This point is related to that discussed immediately above (the Nürnberg Principle), but is separate in that it tasks each individual to be ethical, whether or not commands from a superior are involved.

Within the American military - most conspicuously in the officer corps - there is a further expectation that **professional** ethics be acknowledged and observed. These ethics are couched in terms of one's responsibility to one's service, fellow servicemembers, and country. They do not address ethics beyond the Lockean universe, and indeed it would probably be worrisome to the nation if they did. The armed forces exist to preserve and protect the United States as it is defined by the Constitution, after all - not to presume to judge that definition.

To the extent that American military thinking is thus bounded by Constitutional values, military leaders are uncomfortable venturing outside that ordered environment. Conventional military wisdom is simply to war against and defeat those who think and act in ways that are perceived as an "unacceptable" threat to the

---

[42] *Department of Defense Law of War Manual.* Washington, D.C.: Office of General Counsel, Department of Defense, 2015, page #1, ¶1.1.1.

United States, with the expectation that they will then see the error of their ways and be converted to "right thinking". Persistent rogues will be dispatched. The psychology is essentially similar to that of the medieval Crusades, wherein it was thought entirely proper to win converts to Christianity - or Islam - at swordpoint.

5. Civilian Preeminence

The United States incorporates the principle of civilian superiority to the armed services. The effect of this from an ethical perspective is to place a certain escape-hatch between military leaders and their responsibility to Constitutional values.

While the Nürnberg principle forbids the military to relinquish personal ethical responsibility for their decisions, the civilian government can cite its Constitutional superiority in support of its prerogative to "interpret" said ethics. At the national level it would be unacceptable for a military leader to challenge that presumption [and it must be borne in mind that controversial issues are rarely clear-cut ones where the Constitution is concerned].

As a practical matter the Constitution is what the executive branch of the government **says** it is, except in those occasional instances where what amounts to a "priesthood" of this surrogate divinity - the Supreme Court - assumes the prerogative to **interpret** the Constitution, much in the same way that ancient Egyptian priests sought to interpret the will of Amon-Ra or that medieval scholars sought to interpret Christian scripture through canon law.

6. The Continuing Ethical Challenge

What the four principles discussed above illustrate is that it is no easy matter to determine or apply ethics within the American military culture. Ethics is an elusive concept whose very vagueness leaves the individual uncertain as to just what his actual responsibility is, to say nothing of how he should apply it.

C. PSYOP: "UnAmerican But Necessary"

What does all this have to do with PSYOP?

To be effective in his art, the PSYOPerator **must** venture beyond the Lockean universe, and he **cannot** allow his assessments of competitive universes to be distorted by Lockean faith-based values.

If he condemns a competing ideological universe, such as Marxism, *a priori* simply because it **is** a competitor, he has safeguarded his orthodoxy within the American military culture - but he has also lost the ear of non-Americans who do not look at socio/political/economic reality through Locke-tinted glasses. To be effective and credible, a PSYOP challenge to Marxism must evaluate it rationally and then propose a rational alternative to it which is conceptually and demonstrably superior. To respond only with an indignant denunciation else is merely to indulge oneself in the equivalent of emotional name-calling, which may be satisfying and reassuring but does **not** adjust matters towards the solution of an international/intercultural impasse.

By its very nature, then, PSYOP sticks in the craw of American political culture - and of its conventional military establishment. To reach through the body into the mind with the intent of manipulating it is somehow held to be an "unclean" science, a kind of Black Art practiced by mad scientists - but **not** by straightforward, decent Americans.[43] We have consoled ourselves that we do it not because we want to, but only because the "other side" does it and we have to counter them.[44]

Once you allow a dog to consider it acceptable to attack human beings (for instance burglars), a threshold has been crossed which changes forever the human-dog relationship. The human can never see his dog in quite the same way once it has tasted human flesh. [Presumably the dog also sees humans, including his master, somewhat differently.] Since PSYOP is conspicuously outside the norms of the American military culture, its practitioners also carry something of a taint.

It would be even more of a taint if they were perceived [or allowed] to develop their arcane art to its potential limits, but [until the advent of MindWar] they are not. Like a sentry-dog on a leash, PSYOP is not allowed to "run wild", adjusting values, thoughts, and behavior according to unorthodox and mysterious criteria. It has been placed firmly and decisively in support of "normal/ traditional" military operations as a "combat support"

---

[43] "Psychological Warfare has always rested as an uneasy activity in democracies, even in wartime. It is partly to do with the suspicion that using the mind to influence the mind is somehow unacceptable. But is it more unacceptable to shoot someone's brains out rather than to persuade that brain to drop down their weapon and live?" - Philip M. Taylor, *Munitions of the Mind* (Manchester: Manchester University Press, 2003, 3rd Edition).

[44] "We occasionally do very wicked things, and in our weighing up the moralities we rather go in for dishonest comparisons; after all, you can't compare the ideals of one side with the methods of the other, can you now?" - Control to Alec Leamas, in John Le Carré's *The Spy Who Came In From The Cold* (New York: Pocket Books, 1963).
"[U.S. Army PSYOP includes] unpardonable methods of ideological sabotage including blackmail, provocation, and terror." - T. Belashchenko, "'Black Propaganda' from Fort Bragg" in *Sovetskiy Voin*. Moscow, June 1980, pages 46-47.

element - a "battlefield janitor" of PW's emotional stresses, fears, and susceptibilities.

In practice this has severely limited the effectiveness of military PSYOP as a means to change the ideological and ethical opinions of the enemy; it renders PSYOP useful only as a means to communicate surrender messages to opposing forces on the battlefield, or to issue controlling instructions to civilians in the area. "Orthodox" themes reaching beyond such simple, direct messages are quickly perceived as sloganistic, hence discounted by all but the most primitive audiences. The technique of interviewing captured or surrendering recipients - at the implicit end of a gun-barrel - is unlikely to elicit sincere comments as to the effectiveness of such propaganda; self-interest dictates an answer contrived to be pleasing to the interrogator.

The final disgrace of PSYOP came in 2010, when the Army renamed its Frankenstein's Monster from "PSYOP" to "Military Information Support Operations" (MISO) - fooling no one, of course, except the renamers themselves.

D. Evolution to MindWar Branch

The new MindWar Branch (MWB) not only permanently retires PSYOP/"MISO"'s role as an embarrassing "battlefield janitor", but emplaces it at the very center of future Army operations. Henceforth all Army missions begin with MW campaigns, with PW operations initiated only in the event of MW's failure.

MWB functions as the "controlling brain" of the MW campaign, determining, evaluating, and modifying the subject-situation conditions causing the problem. During the detection, evaluation, and preparation Phases of the campaign (Phases 0-2), it accomplishes this through the means outlined in Sections #F & G of this chapter. Once

and only if sufficient subject adjustment has been accomplished, the on-site human components of the MW campaign - first MetaForce (Chapter #4) and then ParaPolitics (Chapter #5) are inserted. At all times following such insertion, MWB maintains its "umbrella" over the entire environment, further adjusting it as necessary. It does not close this umbrella until all on-site MW assets are removed.

The old PSYOP doctrine called for techniques to induce confusion, fear, and obedience in the face of U.S. PW operations. It made liberal use of secrecy, lies, rumors, deception, and anything else to degrade and demoralize the faceless, human-dignity-undeserving "Enemy". It sought to incite alienation and if possible defection from the Enemy of its soldiers and civilians alike, thus fragmenting the underlying political and social system.

MWB has nothing to do with any of this. It never lies or selectively distorts the truth. It respects every human being as having the same worth, dignity, and right to "life, liberty, and the pursuit of happiness" no matter what his/her nationality or culture. It does not disrupt existing social or cultural institutions. The "Enemy" in MW is never other human beings; it is the problem which has caused such humans to destabilize their behavior dangerously or destructively.

Thus MWB, when conducting a MW campaign, does so actively and continuously **with** influential humans from the subject situation, **not** against them. The result is a solution both understandable by and satisfactory to the native population indefinitely after the MW campaign ceases and all U.S. assets are withdrawn.

We next turn to the operational universe of MWB, and the tools it uses therein. This involves the nature and functioning of human thought processes and the techniques ("Psycontrols" [PC] or PSYCONs) used both separately and in combination to influence these.

E. Thought Architecture

In order to influence and control the human mind, MW must first know how thoughts are inspired and constructed. This requires an identification of the two types of thought emergence: the **unconscious** and the **conscious**. Despite the fact that 95% of thinking is subconscious, most people assume that their opinions, ideas, and conclusions are all conscious decisions.[45] Indeed much of traditional MISO is based upon this assumption: that it is the deliberately-constructed ideas of an audience which are the target. This is why such campaigns are so ineffective.

1. Unconscious Thought

a. Prevalence

When a human perceives a situation, action, and/or other humans, an instant, unconscious framing of the sensation occurs before there is any conscious reaction or evaluation. Indeed it is the very immensity and habituation of this framing that makes it unnoticeable and unremarkable. Thus the sound of gunfire in the vicinity of one's home elicits alarm, while near a military rifle range it would not. Approaching an intersection triggers accustomed expectations of vehicular and pedestrian behavior, the sequencing of traffic lights, and lane/crosswalk pathways.

---

45 Cf. Leonard Mlodinow, Ph.D., *Subliminal: How Your Unconscious Mind Rules Your Behavior* (New York: Pantheon, 2012).

As an individual encounters different surroundings with different inhabitants, instant classification of them takes place; this is sometimes called "instinct" or "assumptions taken for granted".

This picture is also assumed to be common to all who experience it, but it is in fact markedly unique to each individual. The sum total of all one's cultural indoctrination, education, experiences, prejudices, desires, and emotions serves as the lens through which it it is "perceived as reality".

While the concept of unconscious thought extends well back into antiquity, it received its first modern appreciation from the philosopher Immanuel Kant (1724-1804). Bishop Berkeley's **subjective idealism** had held that nothing could be known objectively - that knowledge is limited to subjective impressions. Kant refines this into what is called **critical idealism**, in which human thought is subdivided into **sensation**, **understanding**, and **pure reason**. Sensations and understanding of them and consequences of them can be proven, Kant says, but pure reason (concepts unsupported by sensations) cannot be conclusive. It is "beyond causality". It is the first two processes - sensation and the overlay of understanding upon that sensation - which result in Kant's "construction of reality".

This "reality" contains predispositions concerning physical surroundings, such as one's like or dislike of the terrain, climate, elevation, level of development, etc. It also includes assumptions concerning the population, both individually and *en masse*, of which some are politically and culturally acceptable and others not. For instance race, religion, sex, the role of the genders, slavery, economic systems, and political ideologies are all factors with extremely powerful influence, but about which open discussion is severely constrained by convention and taboo. Identifying and overcoming such taboos are a major challenge to MWarriors not just in Phase 1 but throughout the entire MW campaign. But it is a challenge which cannot be avoided or sanitized if the MW campaign is to succeed.

b. Pattern Thinking

Unconscious, non-deliberate thought manifests itself not in articulated expressions or ideas, but in overlays or "patterns" into which the sensory impressions are placed and assumed to have significance.[46]

So strong are these patterns that it is pointless to think of "reasoning" or "arguing" people out of them. At most individuals or groups can be forced or enticed to not-comply with them temporarily, but as soon as the threat or bribe is removed, the "reality"-patterns will reassert themselves.

Societies frequently see such patterns articulated as traditions, norms, or other expressions of dominant values, often reduced to simplistic dogma, slogans, or ideologies.

2. Conscious Thought

Distinct from the unconscious is consciousness, which accounts for the remaining 5% of human mental activity. It is generally divided into two realms:

---

[46] With a political, social, and cultural context, cf. in particular Valerie M. Hudson, Philip A. Schrodt, & Ray D. Whitmer, *A New Kind of Social Science: The Path Beyond Current (IR) Methodologies May Lie Beneath Them*. Montreal, Quebec, Canada: International Studies Association, March 26, 2004.
http://web.ku.edu/~keds/papers.dir/forecasting.html

a. Algorithmic

Algorithmic thought (Plato's *dianoia*, Hegel's "dialectic idealism") is what is normally understood as logical or observable reasoning: a math problem or the speed of a nearby car. Unlike pattern-thinking, algorithmic thinking is conscious, deliberate, effort-demanding, and transitory: the moment a particular stimulation no longer demands it, an algorithmic thought retreats into increasingly-vague memory, then if sufficiently ignored it eventually disappears.

Traditional MISO propaganda is so ineffective because it is algorithmic; it makes arguments for reasoned behavioral changes, not recognizing nor appreciating the dominant power of the unconscious patterns governing that behavior.

b. Conceptual

Conceptual thought (Kant's "pure reason", Plato's *nœsis*, Nietzsche's "horizon building") begins from the apprehension of one's conscious self as an existential reality: the *ba* of ancient Egypt, the *psyche* of the Greeks, the Golden Flower of the *Tao*, the soul of Judæo-Christianity, identifying, in the words of Dr. Raghavan Iyer, "... not the shadowy self or false egoity which merely reacts to external stimuli. Rather there is that Eye of Wisdom in every person which in deep sleep is fully awake and which has a translucent awareness of self-consciousness as pure, primordial light."

Conceptual thought then extends to ideas, envisions, and expressions radiating creatively from that affirmation. While central to the very essence of humanity and its innate value independent of all utilitarian concerns, the soul is unidentifiable to and untouchable by MW; nor is it of MW concern. It exists in metaphysics, while MW is interested in the unconscious and algorithmic-conscious analysis and control of the mind.

This quality of thought is the subject of the author's companion book *MindStar*.

F. Liminal Methods

The situational participants may be contacted directly and overtly by the MW team, informed of the team's assigned goal, and invited to cooperate in achieving it. If this sounds like an odd, even naïve way to fight a war, consider that many international conflicts are the result of misunderstandings, narrowly-focused vision, and emotional grandstanding. If conflicts can be objectively and comprehensively defined, and the situational condition identified as something whose resolution is advantageous and prestigious to the conflicted participants, that is the simplest and most direct path to completion of that MW-Matrix component.

1. Voluntary Psycontrol (VPC)

If a cooperative consensus cannot be reached, the team must identify the factors preventing it and attempt to correct or remove them. These may be simple or complex, expensive or incidental financially, and/or in or out of the direct control of the target actors. If the MW team can resolve these by its own skill, and with financial/materiel assets accessible to it, it should continue its efforts.

2. Involuntary Psycontrol (IPC)

If a cooperative consensus cannot be created, the MW team proceeds to create consensus by MW technology:

involuntary Psycontrol (IPC) of the enemy actors. IPC takes two forms: Liminal (LIPC) and Subliminal (SLIPC).

3. Liminal Involuntary Psycontrol (LIPC)

a. The Influence Continuum

The primary vehicle for liminal IPC (LIPC) is the Influence Continuum (described in #A.6 above), which supersedes the old Black/Grey/White propaganda methodology and model. A tailored Influence Continuum may be directed towards either the situation participants themselves or other individuals or groups who can influence those participants in the desired direction. Normally the least forceful of the Continuum stages necessary to achieve cooperative stabilization will be employed, and the LIPC component of the MW campaign coordinated with the others towards the common, immediate goal of the *áristos*.

MW LIPC is effective because it first identifies the governing thought patterns, then stimulates individuals' core reality-lenses to interpret them in the desired way. The next evolution in LIPC will be to electronically map thought patterns which have the same impact among all humans sharing them, and to artificially generate and transmit them to target groups through electronic media. [47]

---

[47] Cf. "Neuroscientists Unlock Shared Brain Codes", Medical Press, October 20, 2011.
http://medicalxpress.com/news/2011-10-neuroscientists-brain-codes.html

b. Liminal Involuntary Psycontrol Constriction

Beyond direct LIPC communication, desired courses of action may further be encouraged by the removal or limitation of alternatives. If a conflict entity is considering PW, for instance, constriction of its financial resources and/or military supplies may make this option impractical. Where possible, such choice-constrictions should be done without explanation or publicity, so as not to highlight them as PW threats or actions. The sole purpose of such constrictions is to channel the conflict participants toward a MW solution.

The inverse of alternative constriction - enticements or promises of rewards for LIPC cooperation, such as economic or military aid - should be avoided. Such bribery discredits the LIPC process in the eyes of both participants and onlookers, and opens the door to insincere, *pro forma* results subject to contemptuous discard the moment such bribes are delivered. Rewards for a successful LIPC operation come about naturally and incidentally, in which case respect and appreciation for the LIPC solution will be that much stronger and more durable.

G. Pre-MW "Mind Control" Attempts

The last half of the Twentieth Century saw numerous experiments in thought-control and extrasensory perception (ESP), some sponsored by various U.S. government agencies. Their common characteristic is that they did not work; they were all attempts to control thought at its expression, not its construction. Briefly summarized:

1. MKDELTA/MKULTRA/MKSEARCH

The CIA's and Defense Department's "mind control" experiments of the 1950-70s were an effort to achieve LIPC through drugs and other invasive means, which in the case of drugs resulted only in confusion and disruption of the human brain's neurological functions. This series of programs completely missed the point that thoughts are the manifestation of mental cohesion, not disintegration (which, since it harms the subject, is impermissible in MW).[48]

2. Project Stargate/ESP

Beginning in 1973 first the CIA, then the NSA, and finally DOD embarked upon a $20 million series of "ESP" experiments together with the Stanford Research Institute (SRI).[49] Originally entitled "Project Scanate",[50] in 1995 it was retitled "Project Stargate".[51]

---

[48] Cf. John Marks, *The Search for the "Manchurian Candidate": The CIA and Mind Control* (New York: New York Times Books, 1979). MKULTRA was established by the CIA in 1953 as a successor to the 1952 MKDELTA. Its purpose was to explore various means of controlling human behavior, of which psychedelic drugs such as LSD were merely one option. Cf. Martin A. Lee & Bruce Shlain, *Acid Dreams: The Complete Social History of LSD: The CIA, the Sixties, and Beyond* (Revised Edition) (New York: Grove Press, 1994). In 1965 DOD initiated a successor to MKULTRA named MKSEARCH, which was limited to drug-behavioral modification only. It was terminated in 1973. Cf. *Congressional Record*, Subcommittee on Health & Scientific Research of the Committee on Human Resources, September 20, 1977, "Human Drug Testing by the CIA, 1977".

[49] SRI is not connected with Stanford University.

[50] Inspired by the then-sensational "Watergate".

[51] Inspired by the then-sensational 1994 science-fiction film *Stargate*, though that film did not contain any ESP themes.

Stargate attempted "remote viewing" experiments, which failed due to the simple fact that the transmission of visual information to the brain does not occur outside of the visible electromagnetic spectrum (EMS), approximately 400-790 THz. It is impossible for EMS waves in this range to survive coherently through atmospheric interference at the extensive distances proposed by SRI. Moreover the electrical impulses within the brain are far too weak even to escape the skull, much less travel any distance beyond it.[52]

Meanwhile, unconnected with SRI or the government, the Transformation Project in San Francisco was collecting vast amounts of records and published results of various government and university experiments in the field of ESP from both the Western & Eastern Blocs as well as nonaligned countries. The range and scope of these files far exceeded anything in the CIA/DIA libraries on this topic.[53]

One of the most rigorous and conclusive analyses was conducted in 1977 by E. Balanovski and J.G. Taylor of the Department of Mathematics, King's College, London. The TP files contained detailed reports of their findings,

---

[52] To light a flashlight bulb a human would need to generate about 30 million times his present level of brain current. Unamplified brainwaves can't be detected beyond EEG electrodes pasted on the body, and such detection is far too crude to be "decoded" into coherent visual images. [See, however, recent fMRI technology under #4. Magnetism.]

[53] The Transformation Project was initiated in 1976 by Michael Murphy, founder of the Esalen Institute in Big Sur, James Hickman, and Steve Donovan as a database of over 9,000 files to correlate the world's research on ESP. They had dialogued extensively and exhaustively with Soviet ESP scientists, and traveled widely in the USSR throughout the 1970s. Murphy wrote up the results in thinly-disguised "fiction" such as *Jacob Atabet* (1977) and *An End to Ordinary History* (1982). Cf. Jeffrey J. Kripal, *Esalen* (Chicago: University of Chicago Press, 2007).

including an extensive article in *Nature* magazine #276, November 2, 1978.

After having reviewed previous experiments attempting to test ESP for EM emission, B&T declared their dissatisfaction because of imprecise test conditions, exclusion of parts of the electromagnetic spectrum (EMS), and inadequate write-ups of the results. They determined to cover the entire EMS, and to do so under the most rigorous test conditions possible.

The battery of sensors they assembled included skin electrodes, electrometers, magnetometers, loop antennae, crystal detectors, horn antennae, thermocouples, electric thermometers, infrared detectors, and ultraviolet detectors. Many of these sensors overlapped one another's frequency range, and altogether they covered the entire EMS from 0 to 3×10^5 GHz. Before the first experiment could be conducted, extensive test-running of all these sensors had occurred in order to record and filter out the irrelevant EM "noise" in the test areas, including passing cars and TV/radio station broadcasts. Readings were recorded on strip chart recorders, video tape recorders, and direct photographs of oscilloscope and frequency analyzer screens. The efficiency of this battery of devices was quickly evident, and the study concluded:

> We have tried to detect EM signals emitted by people, and in particular the Fourier spectrum of such signals, to test the reality of ESP phenomena. All experiments failed to yield any unusual EM radiation. It is possible to conceive transmission of EM energy from one person to another, or of emission by one person in a manner undetectable by the apparatus we have used. This would have been so if very brief pulses of EM energy were used in such signaling with times less than the response time of the corresponding apparatus at the frequency used. There are no known mechanisms in the body able to produce such signals at the power levels required to produce the effects. We have also found that humans are insensitive to low levels of EM. A

possible mechanism for such signaling is therefore clearly ruled out for telepathy and distant-viewing. The EM levels emitted to achieve metal-bending [in the microwave range to achieve the desired focusing] are joules, and there is no known mechanism in the body to achieve a peak power output of GW; it is difficult to suppose that this would be possible without severe tissue damage.

Summarily the human brain can by itself neither send nor receive the stuff of which specific thoughts are made - save through the media of the physical senses. Therefore ESP does not occur, nor do purely mental efforts to produce physical effects (psychokinesis/PK). Apparent successes in these fields are either coincidental, the results of non-mental physical phenomena (magnetic fields, gravity, etc.), or deliberate deception by clever stage-magic trickery.[54]

3. Project Jedi

Following a 1980 an article on "psychotronic warfare" appearing in *Military Review*, the journal of the prestigious Command & General Staff College, the Army in 1984 launched a 5-month experiment called "Project Jedi".[55] Named after the *Star Wars* movie knights who were able to perform exotic mental/magical feats, Project

---

[54] The pretensions of stage magicians such as Uri Geller to ESP and PK powers astounded many researchers and government investigators in the 1970-80s, but not other stage magicians. Cf. James Randi, *Flim-Flam: Psychics, ESP, Unicorns, and Other Delusions* (Buffalo, NY: Prometheus Books, 1982).

[55] Alexander, Lt. Colonel John B., "The New Mental Battlefield: 'Beam Me Up, Spock'". Leavenworth, KS: U.S. Army Command & General Staff College *Military Review*, December 1980. Project Jedi was later [amusingly but somewhat inaccurately] caricatured in the book and film *The Men Who Stare At Goats* (in which George Clooney portrayed Alexander). The fabled goats were in fact the rare "fainting" (myotonic) breed, subject to collapsing when stressed.

Jedi sought to use neurolinguistic programming (NLP) as a new way of teaching recruits to fire weapons.[56] This was done through psychological analysis of the thought-patterns of expert shooters as they fired. 23 soldiers were then trained to fire, some according to the NLP "guided imagery" and others per conventional instruction. Training time was reduced almost by half for the NLP group. To the extent that it decreases reaction time to unexpected situations or confrontations, NLP (whether by that or any other name) would be valuable for Special Forces personnel entering an unknown environment, as in MW Phases #0 & #1.

In 1985 forty Army soldiers undergoing Russian language training were divided into two groups, one of which was trained according to a technique called "Suggestopedia". Developed in the 1970s by the Bulgarian psychotherapist Georgi Lozanov, it involved *t'ai ch'i*-like calisthenics, followed by mental relaxation & breathing exercises, followed by "guided imagery" to reduce students' natural resistance to learning. While not unreasonable for normal teaching environments, it would have no application to MW.[57]

---

[56] Neuro-Linguistic Programming (NLP) was a 1970s' concept proposing a connection between the neurological processes ("neuro"), language ("linguistic"), and behavioral patterns that have been learned through experience ("programming"). It was never physiologically validated, and its claimed psychological results may simply be attributed to habit and skill resulting from concentration and repetition, much as a martial art.

[57] In 1985 the Army commissioned a two-year, $425,000 report from the National Research Council, an agency of the National Academy of Sciences. Among the topics reviewed were stress management, biofeedback, accelerated learning, PK, ESP, and "remote viewing". On December 8, 1987 the NRC report, entitled *Enhancing Human Performance*, was released. It concluded that most of the unconventional techniques were "scientifically insupportable", but that sleep-learning, guided imagery, and "super learning" programs were viable.

H. Subliminal Involuntary Psycontrol (SLIPC)

Subliminal LIPC (SLIPC) encompasses the entire spectrum of external influences upon the natural processes of human thought, awareness, alertness, and disposition. These influences are both naturally and artificially adjusted to maximize the subjects' inclination to receive and positively respond to both.

MW LIPC, which relies upon conscious sensory transmission and reception, may be supplemented by subliminal IPC techniques addressing non-conscious receptors of a target actor's mind and body. Here the objective is not to do bodily or mental damage, but rather to incline the target to be more receptive to LIPC.

1. PSYCON #1: *Homo Electromagneticus*

Along with all other matter/energy displacements in the material universe, the human body is a complex electromagnetic (EM) machine, including its thought processes.

Humans, of course, don't normally think of themselves as machines, but as conscious, unique beings. This casts humanity in not a physical but a metaphysical image, and explains both the basis for and the attraction of religions.

In the 1980s breakthrough research in the EM constitution of man began to emerge. Dr. Robert O. Becker, an orthopedic surgeon whose curiosity had been aroused by the regenerative powers of certain animals.[58] He set out to identify and explore the link between EM and living tissue. In doing so he sought out relevant discoveries by fellow scientists:

---

[58] A hydra cut in half will quickly develop into two hydras, for example, and the salamander can completely replace amputated legs and tail - all at once if necessary - as well as its jaw and eye lenses.

Francis Ivanhoe, a pharmacologist and anthropologist at two universities in San Francisco, made a statistical survey of the braincase volume of all known Paleolithic human skulls, and correlated the increase with the magnetic field strength and major advances in human culture during the same period.

Ivanhoe found bursts of brain-size evolution at about 380-340,000 years ago, and again at 55-30,000 years ago. Both periods correspond to major ice ages, the Mindel and Würm, and they were also eras when great cultural advances were made - the widespread domestication of fire by *Homo erectus* in the early Mindel, and the appearance of *Homo sapiens sapiens* (Cro-Magnon peoples) and gradual decline of Neanderthals (*Homo sapiens*) during the Würm.

Two other glaciations in the same time span - the Ganz ca. 1,200-1,050,000 years ago and the Riss ca. 150-100,000 years ago - didn't call forth such obvious advances in human evolution. They also differed from the other two in that the average geomagnetic field intensity was much lower.

Ivanhoe has proposed a direct link from the magnetic field through the growth-hormone regulator pathways in the brain to account for the sharp evolutionary gains. He suggests that part of the hippocampus, a section of the brain's temporal lobe, acts as a transducer of EM energy. A part of the hippocampus called Ammon's horn, an arch with one-way nerve traffic directed by a strong current flow, may read out variations in the field strength, feeding them by a bundle of well-documented pathways called the fornix to the hypothalamus and thence to the anterior pituitary, where growth hormone is produced. It's known that larger amounts of this hormone in pregnancy increase the size of the cerebral cortex and the number of its nerve cells in the offspring, as compared with other parts of the brain.

Ivanhoe also notes that the hippocampus and its connections with the hypothalamus are among the parts of the brain that are much larger in humans than in other primates. The idea gains further support from the fact that neural activity in the hippocampus increases with electrical stimulation and reaches a maximum at 10^{-15} cps, at or slightly above the dominant micropulsation frequency of today's field.[59]

---

[59] Robert O. Becker, M.D. and Gary Selden, *The Body Electric: Electromagnetism and the Foundation of Life* (NY: William Morrow, 1985).

Becker also came across evidence, from both from his own and others' research, that certain kinds of EM radiation (EMR) can either generate or accelerate damage to living organisms. He cited the instance of the Russian researcher, Yuri Kholodov, who found areas of cell death in the brains of rabbits after subjecting them to 100-200 Gauss magnetic fields. The fields were found to have activated stress hormones within the rabbits, but in a way that the rabbits could not consciously sense any stress.

In 1969 Becker was one of the scientists asked by the U.S. Navy to review possible side-effects from Project Sanguine, the Extremely Low Frequency (ELF) transmitter the Navy intended to build in Wisconsin to communicate with nuclear submarines. He observed:

> The only thing sanguine we found was the name ... The antenna would produce an EM field 1 million times weaker than that from a 765-kilovolt power line. It was to broadcast at 45-70 Hz, frequencies close enough to the Earth's micropulsations that living things are very sensitive to them.
>
> Similar fields had been shown to raise human blood triglyceride levels (often a harbinger of stroke, heart attack, or arteriosclerosis), and change blood pressure and brain wave patterns in experimental animals. The generalized stress response, desynchronized biocycles, and interference with cellular metabolism and growth processes were also distinct possibilities.[60]

The essence of the danger posed by EMR to living organisms is that ELF radiation of 30-100 Hz appears to

---

[60] *Ibid.* Dr. Becker's committee recommended that Project Sanguine be shelved pending further data in these problem areas. The Navy marked the report "For Official Use Only" and eventually moved the project to Michigan, renaming it "Project Seafarer". A new review committee was chosen; Becker was not on it. In 1978 the project was redesigned and renamed "Austere ELF", was again the subject of great controversy, and in 1981 again renamed to "Project ELF" and made operational by the Reagan Administration.

interfere with the body's normal biological cycles. Results may include a continuous condition of mild stress throughout the organism, often triggering its various immune and disease-fighting systems. As the body adapts to the ongoing presence of these systems, their combative effect on serious infections and diseases is lessened. EMR can also cause change in strains of bacteria, enhancing their growth and resistance to antibiotics.[61]

Other experiments examined by Becker yielded implications that:

- Microwave exposure can cause decreased energy levels in the brain by inhibiting electron transport chain function in brain mitochondria.

- Even very weak ELF fields, such as that produced by a TV set 60 feet away, can both accelerate and decrease human reaction time.

- A statistical study of suicide events in the vicinity of overhead high-voltage power lines revealed that magnetic fields averaged 22X higher at suicide addresses, and that areas with the strongest fields contained 40X more fatal locations.

- Animals exposed to EMR undergo a variety of blood changes, such as decline in red cell count and hemoglobin concentration, hence oxygen capacity.

_____

[61] This, suggested Becker, might account for the onslaught of "new" diseases since 1950, many of them developing from pathogens previously incapable of inducing disease. Among these: Reye's syndrome, Lyme disease, Legionnaire's disease, AIDS, and Herpes.

- EMR of the sort received by many people in "home" environments may reduce the strength of electrical impulses governing contraction of the heart muscle by as much as 50X.

- There is an increasing body of evidence that cell-division-related diseases, such as cancer, are aggravated by EMR.

- Improperly or inadequately shielded video terminals may be a factor in the extremely high numbers of women computer operators experiencing miscarriages, stillbirths, and birth defects.

In 1985, when humans' exposure to EMR was considerably less than in the "Information Age" of 2012, Becker summarized his findings:

> It may be hard to convince ourselves that something we can't see, hear, touch, taste, or smell can still hurt us so dreadfully. Yet the fact must be faced, just as we've learned a healthy fear of nuclear radiation. Certain scientists, some perhaps acting in a program of deliberate disinformation, keep telling the public that we still don't know whether electropollution is a threat to human health. That's simply not true.[62]

It is clear that if MW is going to reach into the minds of humans (the United States' own MWarriors and the leaders, military, and citizenry of MW-campaign geopolitical areas), EM is an essential key to unlocking and changing them. But it is a key which must be used with the utmost care and precision, lest it create more danger and damage than it prevents.

---

[62] *Ibid.*

2. PSYCON #2: Brainwave Resonance (BWR)

EMR in the brain occurs in waves measured according to cycles per second (Hz). 1-3 Hz = *delta* waves, characteristic of deep sleep. 4-7 Hz = *theta* waves, characteristic of high emotion, violence, and frustration. 8-12 Hz = *alpha* waves, characteristic of meditation, relaxation, and "searching for patterns". 13-22 Hz = *beta* waves, characteristic of frontal brain activity, deliberate effort, and logical thought.

Concerning the EMS, the principle of resonance is:

(1) a vibration of large amplitude in a mechanical or electrical system caused by a relatively small periodic stimulus of the same or nearly the same period as the natural vibration period of the system.

(2) the intensification and enriching of a musical tone by supplementary vibration that is either sympathetically or mechanically induced.

Brain-waves are subject to the principle of resonance. Energy-waves reaching the brain through **any** medium - eyes, ears, or flesh - will tend to induce the brain-waves to cycle at the **same** wavelength. A common example of visual resonance is the seizures that some people experience when exposed to a light flickering at 10 Hz.

The audio spectrum - being the range of sound vibrations which human hearing can consciously detect - is from 15 Hz (bass) to 20,000 Hz (treble). The infrasonic range - 10-15 Hz - is too low to be consciously detected but is nonetheless capable of inducing resonance in the brain. Below infrasound [and sometimes encompassing it] are Extremely Low Frequency (ELF) waves, which are powerful and durable enough to travel through the Earth for communication with submerged submarines.

Brainwave resonance ("BWR") is significant to SLIPC in both passive and active contexts. Passively a human-interactive environment may be permeated with EMS waves at one or more of the BWR ranges, inclining those within it to their induced characteristics without their conscious awareness. Attempting a relaxed, pleasant, cooperative discussion of a mutual problem is more possible in an *alpha* BWR than in a non-BWR one, and much more possible than in a *beta* one. Trying to accomplish anything complex or creative immersed in *delta* is exhausting and fruitless.

This being the case, it is remarkable how much human interactivity occurs in complete ignorance and disregard of BWR conditions. MWarriors should routinely sample any environment in which they intend to work, to detect negative BWR so that it may be neutralized or replaced with positive BWR. When neutralization or replacement is not possible, the MW interaction should be moved to a different, more supportive location.

Active employment of BWR utilizes frequency generators to project desired BWR into a MW operational environment, to adjust the emotions and awareness of all individuals therein. Such generators may be strategic satellite-based platforms which transmit BWR both directly and through intrusion into existing, localized electronic media systems. BWR can, for instance, be inserted into the Internet to be passively and indetectably (absent such sensors) received and radiated by any accessing device, from television station to desktop computer or cellular telephone.

On a more controlled level, MWarriors may carry personal BWR generators to influence just their immediate surroundings. Depending upon the circumstances, this may be done either overtly or covertly.

BWR SLIPC should not be regarded as merely something to "use against" someone else. Rather it is useful to remove antagonistic or disruptive emotions and replace them with receptive and cooperative ones. Here again it is important to remember that MW always redefines "the enemy" as the **problem situation** affecting all of the human participants, not any segment of the participants themselves. Accordingly what BWR SLIPC seeks to do is to place everyone, including the MWarriors themselves, in the same positive BWR range.

It is well that this is so, because it would be next to impossible to shield anyone within a BWR SLIPC environment to its effects. The infrasonic EMS ranges travel through almost any substance, and enter the human body merely by encountering any of its surfaces. Frequency-cancellation earphones might affect BWR entering through the hearing anatomy, but would offer no protection whatever for the body's entire skin surface.

Summarily all MW planning and operations should be carried out within BWR-controlled environments, which requires first their detection and then, as appropriate, their adjustment.

3. PSYCON #3: Magnetism

a. Transcranial Magnetic Stimulation

As the phenomenon of magnetism is integral with electricity, and human mental activity is electric, it is unsurprising to find that magnetic fields, while not affecting the body's metabolism to a significant degree, due to the extremely small amount of ferromagnetic material therein, can influence thought itself.

As discovered through MRI imaging, the area of the brain in which evaluations and opinions about others' beliefs and morality are made is the tempero-parietal junction (TPJ). In 2010 MIT neuroscientists discovered that application of a magnetic field to the right TPJ, by means of a noninvasive technique called transcranial magnetic stimulation (TMS) temporarily disrupts an individual's ability to make judgments based upon previously-learned morality. In effect, pre-indoctrination is suppressed, resulting in the subject's tending to judge situations more on a discrete cause-and-effect basis. In theory, TMS could be used to condition personnel to make decisions unencumbered by prior moral, social, or ethical indoctrination; and to remove that same protective indoctrination from a hostile individual being interrogated. TMS thus approaches in scientific reality the mythical "brainwashing" of classic conspiracy legend.[63]

The present limitations of TMS from a MW perspective are that its effects are only temporary, and that the magnetic field needs to be precisely created in close proximity to the TPJ. The establishment of a direct cause-and-effect relationship between magnetism and morality, however, opens the MW door to the long-sought "holy grail" of SLIPC: the removal of preexisting moral beliefs.

Unlike BWR, magnetic fields can be generated and focused directionally, in precisely-calculated strengths. A precisely-configured TMS field directed at hostile humans motivated by intense moral conditioning (as in a deeply-held religious belief or irrational political ideology) can instantly dismantle or at least substantially

---

[63] Cf. Anne Trafton, "Moral Judgments Can Be Altered By Magnets", *MIT News*, March 30, 2010 (http://web.mit.edu/newsoffice/2010/moral-control-0330.html).

weaken this barrier to communication and situational reasoning.

The 1990s'-emergent technique of Functional Magnetic Resonance Imaging (fMRI) opens new potential for both the reading of human thoughts and the implantation of them. In fMRI magnetic sensors detect blood-flow activity within the brain with such precision and accuracy that the result can be used by a computer to assemble an accurate image of the subject's visualization from a database of standardized components. In reverse, fMRI may eventually be able to transmit them.[64]

b. Magnetic Reconnection Portals

While MW has occasion to operate at close, interpersonal range where localized magnetic field generators and detectors can be utilized, MW's primary function is on the mass/distance level. Can the forces and principles of magnetism be applied here? Indeed they can, but science is only now coming to the threshold of this environment and its potential.

The Earth is, among other things, an all-enveloping magnet. Most humans know about its poles, which enable compasses to function; but less well-known is the array of ultra-low-frequency (ULF) waves stretching around the planet between them, forming an electromagnetic network or sheet of ionized gases called the **MagnetoSphere** (MS).

The MS is the product not only of Earth's own magnetic field waves, but of those projected by the Sun -

---

[64] Cf. Thomas Naselaris et al., "Bayesian Reconstruction of Natural Images from Human Brain Activity", *Neuron 63*, September 24, 2009, pages #902-15.

the "Solar Wind" (SW) - and the plasma which comprises about 99% of the observable universe.[65]

In 2012 NASA announced that a system of "portals" had been identified wherein the MS and SW connect and interact, producing magnetic storms and other atmospheric irregularities. In 2015 NASA launched the Magnetospheric MultiScale (MMS) mission, consisting of four spacecraft to study the magnetic reconnection (MR) properties of these portals. MRPs link the Sun's magnetic field lines to those of the Earth, releasing gigantic bursts of energy (the Auroræ Borealis & Australis being one such phenomenon). As these MRPs become predictable, calculable, and mapped, MWarriors may be able to apply their magnetic fields and waves to the emotions and thought-patterns of humans within their range.[66]

4. PSYCON #4: Chronobiology

Chronobiology ("CB") is the science of the influence of states and periods of time upon biological entities. CB oscillations - the "ticking of biological clocks" - occurs at an extensive number of levels in the human body, from the cellular to the entire organic body, and at velocities from the milliseconds to the multiples of years.

MW is concerned primarily with the CB attuned to and governed by the solar ("circadian") day. It is this entrainment which makes the MWarrior's mind and body more or less efficient, and the MW subjects more or less receptive and controllable.

---

[65] These ULF-waves are also called "Alfven Waves" in honor of Hannes Alfven, who received the 1970 Nobel Prize for their discovery.

[66] One speculative example of how MRPs could be accessed to amplify BWR on a continental scale with minimum need of operator-generated energy is given in the author's MW novel *We Break the Sword* (2016).

Some of the human body's various circadian cycles are immediately and strongly determined by and sensitive to sensory environmental changes. A well-known example is the "jet lag" disorientation and exhaustion experienced when one is rapidly displaced from one day/ night standard to another.[67]   Similar effects may be produced by the removal of sensory circadian reinforcement, such as seclusion in a windowless room without a clock, or extended immersion in sensory-deprivation tanks. The more detection and reinforcement supports are removed, the more quickly disorientation and psychosis result.[68]

Nevertheless it is not the purpose of MW to disrupt or destroy mental coherence, but rather to make operatives most alert and efficient at what they do, and their audiences most receptive and impressionable to the MW campaign.

Human circadian phase response curves ("PRC") are generally established for the individual's awake/sleep cycle, as these are the most regular, obvious, and recurrent divisions. Within a waking period individuals can vary uniquely, though alertness is generally highest after transition from sleep and lowest just prior to the next transition to sleep. Politicians, for example, know that it is best to handle interviews demanding mental alacrity in the morning, while scheduling prepared

---

[67] Cf. Till Roenneberg, *Internal Time: Chronotypes, Social Jet Lag, and Why You're So Tired* (Cambridge: Harvard University Press, 2012). The author is Professor at the Institute of Medical Psychology at the Ludwig-Maximilians University, Munich.

[68] Cf. John C. Lilly, M.D., *The Deep Self* (New York: Warner Books #33-023, 1977). Lilly was the principal proponent of, and experimenter with the sensory deprivation tank during the 1960s-70s, herein summarizes and analyzed the findings of his earlier books and reports, and offers practical guidance concerning the construction and use of isolation tanks. Lilly, along with his work was portrayed in Paddy Chayefsky's 1978 novel [& 1980 film] *Altered States* (New York: Harper Collins, 1978).

speeches for late in the day when audiences are most vulnerable and passive. As Adolf Hitler wryly observed:

> A speaker knows that even the time of day his speech is given is important in determining its effectiveness. The same speech, speaker, and subject produce completely different responses at ten in the morning, at three in the afternoon, and in the evening ... To make it easy for everyone to attend, I set the meeting for a Sunday morning at ten. The result was catastrophic but extremely instructive. The hall was full and the decor stunning, but audience response was glacial. Nobody was enthusiastic, and I was profoundly disappointed at failing to establish any relationship, not even the slightest connection, with my audience.[69]

Prior to any MW team insertion into a given geographical area, all team personnel should have their CB PRCs adjusted to that location, which can be done through a variety of entrainments, such as Melatonin and controlled light exposure. MW actions designed to impact local individuals, groups, or general populace should also be timed for the CB PRC of greatest receptivity where possible.

5. PSYCON #5: Proxemics

Proxemics refers to the interrelated observations and theories of man's use of space as a specialized elaboration of culture.[70] It rejects the usual assumption that all sensory experiences are commonly shared by humans subject to them. People from different cultures inhabit substantially different sensory worlds of conditioned filtering of significant/irrelevant information.

---

[69] Adolf Hitler, *Mein Kampf* (Volume II). Munich: Franz Eher, 1926.

[70] Edward T. Hall, *The Hidden Dimension*. Garden City: Doubleday & Co., 1966.

Proxemics is easily recognizable in nonhuman animals, who all have a flight distance ("FD"): the point at which it will flee when approached by a potential predator. Within the FD is the critical distance ("CD"), which, if reached, will trigger the animal to stalk or attack the intruder:

> A lion in a zoo will flee from an approaching man until it meets an insurmountable barrier. If the man continues the approach, he soon penetrates the lion's CD, at which point the cornered lion reverses direction and begins to stalk the man. In the classical animal act in the circus, the lion's stalking is so deliberate that he will surmount an intervening obstacle such as a stool in order to get at the man. To get the lion to remain on the stool, the lion-tamer quickly steps beyond the CD. At this point the lion stops pursuing. The trainer's elaborate "protective" devices - the chair, the whip, or the gun - are so much window-dressing. - H. Hediger, animal psychologist[71]

Human beings also possess FD/CD, as well as an intermediate personal and social distance ("PSD"). Individuals make FD/PSD/CD decisions by sight, hearing, and smell at a distance; and touch up close. In some cultures people are accustomed to being within the smell-radius of others, and in fact judge moods, class, and relationships in part on olfactory impressions. In other cultures, such as that of the United States, the scent of anyone except an intimate is repellent.[72]

The human skin's ability to both transmit and sense emotional states is greater than most people realize. Anger or embarrassment triggers blushing, but it also increases the blood supply to various parts of the body, causing [among other things] subtle swelling of the

---

[71] Hall, *op.cit.*

[72] This creates an invisible yet powerful barrier against American rapport with various Mideastern, Asian, and African societies.

forehead and temples, and increased skin temperature in those areas. Observers can detect such changes by skin-based thermal detectors, by more intense olfactory sensation (smell), and by visual impact.[73]

Heat and space are related. People in a cool, crowded room will not feel as cramped as in a hot one.[74]

Even photographs and paintings of people create an immediate attitude-impression in a viewer whom they place in FC/PSD/FD of the subject.[75] [76]

The boundary of each human does not end with the skin. Each individual possesses an unseen "personal field" - or rather variety of them - which constitutes his or

---

[73] Some women interviewed by Hall commented that changes in the bodily temperature and odor of dancing partners, for example, were reliable advance-signs of lust, anger, etc. - long before the male in question would speak or act accordingly.

[74] Whether or not you see or hear other persons, your heat-sensors will react to them if you are close enough. To sample your own heat-radiation sensitivity, place the back of your hand close to your lips. Both generate a high level of heat. Then move your hand up and down in front of your face.

[75] Four to eight feet is the portrait distance: Here the painter is near enough so that his eyes have no trouble in understanding the sitter's solid forms, yet he is far enough away so that the foreshortening of the forms presents him no real problems. Here, at the normal distance of social intimacy and easy conversation, the soul of the sitter begins to appear. Nearer than three feet, within touching distance, the soul is far too much in evidence for any sort of disinterested observation. Three feet is the sculptor's working distance, not the painter's. The sculptor must stand near enough to his model to be able to judge forms by sense of touch. - Maurice Grosser, *The Painter's Eye* (NY: Rinehart & Co.).

[76] The Renaissance rediscovered perspective, enabling a viewer to see various parts of a painting proportionately. Rembrandt painted "stationary visual fields", such that by focusing on a portrait's central feature the viewer sees the entire portrait in the same clarity/lack of clarity as if standing before the individual in question and observing him/her with foveal, macular, and peripheral vision.

her true boundary. The MWarrior who first detects, then control such personal fields thus controls the subject individuals as assuredly as if controlling their conscious personalities.

6. PSYCON #6: Atmospheric Ionization

A negatively-ionized atmosphere induces relaxation, alertness, energy, and a general sense of well-being in humans who breathe it [only as long as they continue to breathe it]. By contrast exposure to a positively-ionized atmosphere induces lethargy, exhaustion, irritability, and confusion. In a MW campaign, therefore, it is useful to negatively-ionize the atmosphere not only in the subject geographical area, but in MW facilities themselves.

Here it is important to distinguish positively/ negatively-ionized air (as a   result) from ionizing radiation (as a cause). Normal atoms consist of an equal number of positively-charged protons [in addition to non-charged neutrons] and orbiting, negatively-charged electrons. An ion is any atom or molecule with a greater number of electrons (negative ion = *anion*) or a lesser amount (positive ion = *cation*). Such imbalances are caused by external radiation strong enough to disrupt the atom. It is ionizing radiation which accounts for the damage to humans from nuclear bombs: *alpha*, *beta*, *gamma*/X-ray, and neutron.[77]

The air humans breathe contains varying mixtures of atoms, anions, and cations. "Air ionizers" do not create ions by radiation; rather they generate an electrical field which causes cations to ground, leaving the air and attaching themselves to the earth or other grounded substances. Consequently a human in the vicinity will

---

[77] These designations are unrelated to the brainwave frequencies discussed elsewhere in this work.

breathe a higher percentage of anions, causing the beneficial sensations.

Naturally-occurring anionic atmosphere can be caused by electrical discharge (such as lightning) or fast-moving water molecules (rainstorms, waterfalls, sea waves, etc.). As such events can be predicted, or such areas identified, MW should take advantage of them to condition the mental dispositions of individuals subject to them.

Cationic air results from dry atmospheric conditions and winds, most significantly **katabatic** and **rain shadow** winds. A katabatic wind (such as the California *Santa Ana*, Adriatic *Bora*, Japanese *Oroshi*) is a wind that carries high-density air from a higher elevation down a slope under the force of gravity. Shadow winds (such as the Alpine *Föhn* and South African *Bergwind*) result when air driven upslope on the windward side of a mountain range loses its moisture before descending on the far side.

Cationic air can also be caused by any high-velocity abrasion, such as rough surfaces and sharp angles in air-conditioning or ventilating systems.

All MW environments, both planning/operational and subject area, should be pretested for ionization and adjusted [or the people relocated] to the anionic insofar as possible. Within closed areas artificial "ionizers" can be overtly or covertly employed, and in open areas devices for creating favorable atmospheric conditions (e.g. rainstorms) may be both strategically and tactically employed.

Insertion of a MetaForce team into a subject location, for instance, should be preceded and accompanied by an anionic "blanket", for the safety and efficiency of the team itself as well as for the receptive conditioning of persons or groups it encounters.

7. PSYCON #7: Color

In conventional PSYOP colors are used culturally and socially with respect to target audiences. Thus while black is the color of death in the American/European countries, white represents it in China, India, Vietnam, and Korea; and so on.

While not ignoring such traditional connotations, MW is more concerned with color as it directly impacts and influences the human brain as EMR. The inclusive scientific discipline is that of photobiology: the study of the effects of light on biological systems.

The EMS ranges from a theoretical "long wave" the length of the universe to short, high-frequency waves a fraction of the size of an atom. While the extremes of the EMS are theoretically infinite, for practical scientific measurement the range extends from 0 Hz (hertz = cycles per second) to 10 picometers (a picometer being a trillionth of a meter). Within this vast range of EMR the conscious human senses can detect only the tiny ranges of visible light, heat, and audible sound.

Visible light is the color spectrum, from red to violet. It occupies the tiny segment of the EMS from 400-790 THz, EMR capable of exciting the retinal molecules of the human eye. In fact humans can see only three actual colors: red, green, and blue - because the retina contains photoreceptors for just those colors.

The ability to distinguish between range of colors is made possible by a protein called **opsin**. Opsin separates the pigments on the color wavelengths that passes through the cones or photoreceptors present in the eye in order to distinguish one from the other. The "red" photoreceptor in the eye actually detects yellow light, but the brain remaps the yellow-green differential signal to red.

Thus humans are **trichromats**. All of the other colors humans think they "see" are actually the result of their brains evaluating and constructing various red/green/blue mixtures.[78]

There are nonhuman animal species who are dichromats (seeing only two colors) or monochromats (seeing only one). This is generally presumed to be the result of genetic adaptation to environment, such as nocturnal or underwater existence. Some species of birds and fish are tetrachromats, being able to see ultraviolet.

MW, therefore, is interested essentially in the direct brain impacts of these three actual color EMRs, and only incidentally in what habitual or cultural play various brains make of them.

Red EMR provokes faster and more forceful responses in humans, regardless of their cultural conditioning. For this reason it can also be counterproductive in situations requiring complex mental or motor skills.[79] Blue stimulates alertness and creativity. Green reduces alertness and memory.[80] MW planning & operational environments, as well as subject areas, should be illuminated and/or shielded accordingly depending upon the desired mental attitude. Note here that, as visible

---

[78] This is why a color television set, for example, contains only red, green, and blue projectors, and, incidentally/amusingly, why the Martians of the classic 1953 film *War of the Worlds* had "monstrous" red/green/blue eyes. Cf.
http://www.cedmagic.com/featured/war-worlds/war-of-the-worlds.html

[79] Cf. Andrew J. Elliot & Henk Aarts, "Perception of the Color Red Enhances the Force and Velocity of Motor Output", *Emotion*, Vol 11(2), April 2011, 445-449.

[80] G. Vandewalle, C. Schmidt, G. Albouy, V. Sterpenich, A. Darsaud, G. Rauchs, P.-Y. Berken, E. Balteau, C. Degueldre, A. Luxen, P. Maquet, D.J. Dijk, "Brain Responses to Violet, Blue, and Green Monochromatic Light Exposures in Humans : Prominent Role of Blue Light and the Brainstem", *PLoS One*, 11/28/2007.

light is a range within the EMS, transmission of that frequency to the audience is all that is required; visually "seeing" it is not. While the human eye's photoreceptors are triggered by red, green, or blue frequencies, they may also be absorbed into the brain through the ears or skin.

Control of color also affects MWarriors' powers of evaluation and reaction in unexpected situations. Humans make subconscious judgments about encountered persons, objects, or environments within 90 seconds of perceiving them, and color sensation accounts for over 60% of that judgment.[81]

8. PSYCON #8: Shapes

Humans are subconsciously influenced by their apprehension of certain shapes or patterns in objects or pictures. This refers back to the previously-discussed "pattern thinking" phenomenon, and is essentially a categorization of its components.

Since the natural tendency of human perception is to unconsciously recognize, classify, and disregard the vast amount of routinely-encountered visual input, anything intended to seize and hold a passive subject's attention must fulfill what the photographer William Mortensen called the "command to look" (CTL).[82] The CTL consists of three elements: impact, subject interest, and participation.

The impact of an image is not intellectual, but biological and subconscious: It is essentially a reaction to the sudden perception of "danger", signaled by certain

---

[81] Cf. Dr. Morton Walker, *The Power of Color*; Avery Publishing Group, 1991; and Ronald E. Green, *The Persuasive Properties of Color*, Marketing Communications, October 1984.

[82] William Mortensen, *The Command to Look: A Formula for Picture Success*. San Francisco: Camera Craft Publishing Company, 1937.

shapes, angles, or patterns which are inherently alarming and destabilizing. There are four basic types of these:

1. The **diagonal**, e.g. the lightning bolt = something that moves swiftly with determination.

2. The **S-curve**, e.g. the snake (something that approaches in a **slithering** fashion) or the curves of the body (especially female = "the line of beauty").

3. **Triangle** combinations, e.g. a blade, sharp points, or teeth (= the threat of **sharpness**).

4. Compact **dominant mass**, e.g. large animal or trapezoid (= massive block in one's path).

A constructed MW image will contain combinations of these, included with or integrated within the superficial image, to seize and hold the viewer's attention.

Perhaps the most striking illustration of such techniques was the German Expressionist cinema of the early 20th century. As Lotte Eisner observes concerning the 1919 classic *Cabinet of Dr. Caligari*:

> Oblique, curving, or rectilinear lines converge across an undefined expanse towards the background: a wall skirted by the silhouette of Cesare the somnambulist, the slim ridge of the roof he darts along bearing his prey, and the steep paths he scales in his flight. In *Expressionismus und Film* Rudolf Kurtz points out that these curves and slanting lines have a meaning which is decidedly metaphysical. For the psychic reaction caused in the spectator by oblique lines is entirely different from that caused in him by straight lines. Similarly, unexpected curves and sudden ups and downs provoke

emotions quite different from those induced by harmonious and gentle gradients. But what matters is to create states of anxiety and terror. The diversity of planes has only secondary importance.

In Gustav Meyrink's *Golem* the houses in the Prague ghetto, which have sprouted like weeds, seem to have an insidious life of their own "when the autumn evening mists stagnate in the streets and veil their imperceptible grimace".

In some mysterious way these streets contrive to abjure their life and feelings during the daytime, and lend them instead to their inhabitants, those enigmatic creatures who wander aimlessly around, feebly animated by an invisible magnetic current. But at night the houses reclaim their life with interest from these unreal inhabitants; they stiffen, and their sly faces fill with malevolence. The doors become gaping maws and shrieking gullets.

"The dynamic force of objects howls their desire to be created," Kurtz declared, and this is the explanation of the overpowering obsessiveness of the *Caligari* sets.[83]

Once attracted, that attention must be changed to interest, which is accomplished by the excitement of emotional pattern-thinking. The strongest of such themes are sex, sentiment, and wonder - the time-tested staples of the entertainment and advertising industries.[84] In MW it is simply a matter of including one or more of these features in the image or message.

---

[83] Lotte H. Eisner, *The Haunted Screen*. Berkeley: University of California Press, 1965.

[84] "It is interesting to note," comments Mortensen, "that women are just as much attracted to the theme of sex when presented in the form of the female nude as men are. Their attraction in this case is vicarious, rather than direct. Their pleasure comes in **imagining** themselves placed in a situation where they would receive the same admiration that goes out to the theme of the picture." The sentiment-theme is usually effected through the softer aspects of sex, children, hardships of humble life, domestic life, animals, landscapes, national pride, glamour of the past, etc. The wonder-theme is quite broad and covers the areas of unknown, uncertain, mysterious things, as well as themes of the supernatural, the macabre, etc.

Finally, and of course most importantly in MW, the viewer's perception of reality, and consequent behavior, must be transformed by exposure to the attraction of the image. This third CTL element - participation - results from the inclusion of geometric alignments which draw the eye of the viewer along and into the constructed patterns, making them indistinguishable from what the viewer subconsciously considers to be his original values, opinions, and dispositions.[85]

9. PSYCON #9: Hypnotism

Hypnotism (after the Greek god of sleep, Hypnos) became popularized in the West in the 19th century as a consequence of interest in Asian meditative practices, e.g. Yoga. There followed a century of confusion and experimentation both comical and sinister, as in the CIA's ARTICHOKE and MKULTRA efforts to create amnesiac assassins a la *The Manchurian Candidate*.[86] Opportunistic therapeutic and stage-entertainment venues, often difficult to distinguish from one another, have been built up around it, and the claims for its efficacy are indeed mesmerizing.

The reality is both less fanciful and more practically useful to the MWarrior. As discussed above, ordinary human sensory awareness is a combination of 95% unconscious impressions and 5% conscious ones. The result is a *tsunami* of sensations combining to create the

---

[85] In constructing Disneyland, Walt Disney imagineered Main Street to have gently-curved, not sharply-angular streetcorners. Both the Main Street buildings and Sleeping Beauty's Castle also incorporate the principle of "forced perspective", with the scaling of each higher level proportionately reduced to make each structure appear taller than it actually is.

[86] Cf. Marks, *op.cit.*, Chapter 11 "Hypnosis". Cf. also the previous discussions here of Projects MKULTRA and Jedi.

individual's state of mind at any moment. By an effort of concentration, controlled by either oneself (meditation, autosuggestion) or an outside source (a human "hypnotist" or EMS device), this state of constant confusion and distraction can be reduced to "background noise" in favor of a more dominant, constant, and attractive stimulus. The individual is not sent into a state of unconscious (*delta*) sleep, but rather into an *alpha* state of receptive relaxation.[87] The "hypnotizing" visual object, sound, or other compelling stimulus becomes and remains the center of attention, and along with this attention comes a tendency to automatic compliance with it, or with any variations in it (once again the above-discussed principle of resonance at work). Once the stimulus ceases, its memory will remain with the subject, in varying degrees of influence.

This is the actual principle behind audio/visual entertainment media advertising. Watching a television show induces an *alpha* state of relaxed belief and trust in what one is seeing and hearing. When the program shifts to a commercial message, it impacts that same *alpha* state, impressing itself on the viewer more effectively than possible were he or she to see or hear the same sales message while in a fully awake and critical *beta* state.

"Being in a state of hypnosis" also allows for fraud on the part of both hypnotist and subject: The hypnotist can issue or commands or give suggestions that he knows will not be obeyed subconsciously/involuntarily, but simply per the subject's *alpha*-passive willingness to believe and cooperate. The subject responds for the same relaxed/willing reason - because to resist would require a return to the less-pleasant, more demanding *beta* alertness.

---

[87] Cf. Benjamin Kissin, M.D., "Conscious and Unconscious Programs in the Brain" (*Psychobiology of Human Behavior*, Volume 1) (New York: Plenum Medical Books, 1986).

What the phenomenon of "hypnotism" means to the MWarrior, then, is simply that insistent, demanding, repeated messages or themes have a crowding-out effect on an audience's ordinary mental sensations, and that [as Adolf Hitler observed in *Mein Kampf*, cited in "Chronobiology" above] a relaxed, tired audience is already *alpha*-receptive to them beyond their intrinsic logic.

10. PSYCON #10: Martial Artistry

The important thing in the martial arts is not to win; it is to survive. The most vital techniques in *Budo* are those which preserve life. That is why the ultimate secret of the martial arts is said to be "to win without fighting".
- Masaaki Hatsumi, Ph.D.
34th Grandmaster, Togakure-ryu Ninjutsu
Founder of the Bujinkan System

The oriental martial arts are commonly regarded as a means of skilled physical combat - which indeed they are in their most conspicuous public image. If one takes the time and effort to study the ideas underlying them, however, a substantially different perspective emerges: that of combat as a last resort after resolution of a confrontation cannot be achieved nonviolently.

This is not a question of argumentative skills, but rather of body language and a personal presence commanding and calming the tension of an encounter. This is achieved by sufficient education and training in both the physical skills and ethical philosophy of martial artistry.[88]

---

[88] Cf. Masaaki Hatsumi, *The Way of the Ninja: Secret Techniques* (Tokyo: Kodansha International, 2004); Jack E. Hoban, *The Ethical Warrior* (Spring Lake, New Jersey: RGI Media, 2012); and David Carradine, *The Spirit of Shaolin* (Boston: Charles E. Tuttle, 1991).

In a MW campaign Phases 0 and 3, MetaForce teams will be on the ground in the geographic area in question, interacting directly with disputing groups and individuals. In Phase 4 ParaPolitics teams will be in the same setting, albeit with the threat of imminent PW alleviated. In any of these situations the presence and brandishing of PW weapons would obviously be counterproductive. If carried, they should be concealed, and their display as a threat or their actual use is to be avoided wherever possible. The chances for such avoidance are substantially increased if all MF and PP personnel are trained and conditioned to react to confrontations as Ninja.

11. PSYCON #11: Fields

As discussed in PSYCON #1, the human body is an electromagnetic machine. As such it both generates and is enveloped by EM fields (EMF), controlling everything from heartbeat and respiration to sleep and female menstrual cycles.

External to the human body, of course, are a great many natural and artificial EMFs, some (such as the Earth's geomagnetic field) quite substantially larger. Both larger and smaller external EMFs may be weak or strong, and at every instant each human within their range is subject to not just their several effects but combined ones as well. EMFs are subject to the principle of **entrainment**, which essentially means that a weaker field exposed to a stronger one will tend to align with it; and even a weaker field, if constant, may entrain a stronger but intermittent or irregular one.

To understand the significance of EMFs to the human body, it is first necessary to appreciate that each such body is not an inert, static clump of permanent matter. It is rather an organic complex in a constant state of reorganization and reconstitution. For instance, human liver and serum proteins are replaced every 10 days, and the whole of the proteins in the body about every 160 days. Moreover these protein molecules are extremely complex devices, not mere raw material; not even a single amino acid can be out of place in the replacement.

To put it another way, there are about 60 thousand billion cells in the human body, and every day about 500 billion of these die and are replaced and rebuilt.

Why? One possibility is that these molecules are so complex that they are inherently unstable and thus are continuously deteriorating. The metabolic system, including the liquid-based transmission of food and raw material throughout the body, is a raging furnace of consumption and regeneration.

How does the body know precisely how to recreate each cell and molecule? It cannot be **within** the object itself, because an object cannot "organize itself". The answer lies in the existence of an entire layered network of EMFs throughout and within the body, altogether comprising a "master plan" EMF for it. Dr. Harold Saxon Burr, Professor Emeritus of Anatomy, Yale School of Medicine, named this the **L-Field** (for "Life-Field"/LF).[89]

What exactly **is** a "field"? When something occurs somewhere in space because something else happens somewhere else in space, by no detectible means by which the cause produces the effect, the two events are said to be connected by a "field" [well-known examples being gravity and magnetism].

In the case of the human body, its organizing system cannot be chemical, because then that system itself would be subject to the same entropic process. Hence there is more to a human being than mere chemistry. It requires

---

[89] Harold Saxon Burr. M.D., *The Fields of Life: Our Links with the Universe*. New York: Ballantine Books #23559, 1972.

an **organizing field**, not merely an accidental accumulation of proteins; thus the notion of "gene randomness" is invalid.

Organization inherently requires **preconception based upon purpose**. Thus human physical existence **has** purpose; it is not accidental. The ancient Greeks identified this as the principle of teloç (*telos*), signifying the inherent end, function or purpose of every phenomenon. [Its most famous modern refutation is Existentialism, which denies not only any purpose to individual entities, but indeed to existence itself.]

Anything that can organize must necessarily exist **before** what it organizes. DNA, for instance, contains "building block" codes, but not the "plan" or motivating force to organize an entire human body out of these "blocks".

If LFs are a natural constant phenomenon, this would account for the general cessation of human physical evolution at least 100,000 years ago [and possibly much longer], as well as for the basic commonality of all human physical construction. Simple Darwinism is inadequate to explain the extreme complexity of higher life, such as development of such mechanisms as Darwin himself called "evolutionary novelties" - the eye and various complex organs. Additionally any such "novelties" would have to occur **simultaneously** for the whole organism to work together. The odds against this are so high that evolutionists simply bypass the question.

Where MW is concerned, LFs are important because their preservation or disruption immediately/similarly affects the humans within and controlled by those fields. PSYCONs #2 and #3 discuss electrical and magnetic wave phenomena as separate variables; this PSYCON #11 focuses on the entire mix of fields (EM&L) defining, sustaining, and governing each human being, as well as groups of them as extensive as the fields themselves.

Identify the field "definition" of each group, and individual elements of it causing discord, destructiveness, or other negative social/behavioral impulse, can be positively corrected. Even more interesting to MW is the theory that **thought itself** exhibits properties of a field-phenomenon.[90]

Consider the ability to add 2+2. Like the rest of the human body, the nervous system is also constantly disintegrating and regenerating. So the material of brain cells and connecting nerves may have been completely renewed about 100 times since an adult was first taught addition. As he hasn't been taught addition all over again 99 times, how does he **still** know how to add?

This is a question not of mere memory, but of the structure of thought organization and integrity. The interaction and entrainment of such "T-fields" (TF) may account for individuals' abilities to sense, emulate, or inculcate moods, impulses, desires, and fears in others, both individually and *en masse*.[91] Just as LFs are distinct from the physical body they create and organize, so TFs are superior to and separate from the physical machinery they manipulate and use.[92] That TFs also have the ability to entrain LFs may explain the well-known phenomena of mental states affecting bodily harmony and health, and vice-versa, as when bodily energy affects mental alertness.

---

[90] This extrapolation of Dr. Burr's concept of LFs was proposed by Edward W. Russell in his *Design for Destiny* (New York: Ballantine Books #23405, 1971).

[91] Thus the mysterious human emotional force of "love" may be in effect the entrained harmony of two individuals' TFs.

[92] The phenomena of "ghosts" may thus be the persistence of TFs past the human bodies they previously defined, and "haunted houses" their continued presence in surroundings familiar to them.

In this model, therefore, the brain is properly seen as the mechanism used by one's primary and subordinate TFs for the cataloguing of sensory input and the storage of memory. These are **results, not** the thing itself, of the self-aware "thinker", the primary TF which is individual consciousness of identity and being.

Sensory areas of the brain are more or less permanently wired to the respective physical senses, hence their injury or loss is quantifiable and somewhat irreparable. But learning and memory functions are not so localized, as long as enough brain cells remain to be usable. These are used only intermittently and at desire or need.

This is why memory is so subtle and elusive a thought-activity. Memory is the backbone of one's current situation. It is how one **conveniently** decides who he is and communicates that to others. But it is still **not** the nucleus of the conscious self. It is this ultimate self which is **the thing that assigns meaning and value to both memory and current sensations**:

> I'm a man in search of his true self. How archetypically American can you get? **Everybody's** looking for his true self. We're all trying to fulfill ourselves, understand ourselves, get in touch with ourselves, get ahold of ourselves, face the reality of ourselves, explore ourselves, expand ourselves. Ever since we dispensed with God, we've got nothing but **ourselves** to explain this meaningless horror of life. We're all weekending at est or meditating for forty minutes a day or squatting on floors in a communal OM or locking arms in quasi-Sufi dances or stripping off the deceptions of civilized life and jumping naked into a swimming pool filled with other naked searchers for self. Well, I think that **true** self, that **original** self, that **first** self, is a real, mensurate, quantifiable **thing**, tangible and incarnate. And I'm going to **find** the fucker!
> - Edward Jessup, Ph.D. (after several glasses of wine)[93]

---

[93] Chayefsky, Paddy, *Altered States* (New York: Harper & Row, 1978).

12: PSYCON #12: Magic

These aren't the droids you're looking for.
- Obi-wan Kenobi, *Star Wars*

Magic, as studied and employed by professional magicians, consists not only of stage props and physical dexterity, but also of misdirection, deception, and sensory preemption. The effect, normally just for entertainment, is to make the seemingly-impossible happen, right before the eyes of an astonished audience.

Less ethically and benignly, magic has been used by confidence men to sting their marks, by generals to overcome their enemies[94] , by religious leaders to sway the credulous, and by politicians to get elected to office.

Common to magic generally are these factors:

a. **Either control of the environment or adaptation of the magic to it.** Only the simplest "table tricks" of magic can be done without regard to their surroundings. For most illusions to be effective, the complete environment in which they are activated must be controlled: lighting, absence or presence of external noise, intentional distractions from close attention, audience alertness and receptiveness. While an illusion is intended to appear spontaneous, it frequently requires careful advance preparation out of view of the eventual audience.

b. **Establishment of the magician's dominant relationship.** The magician displays a *persona* - dress,

---

[94] The U.S. Army's current menu of deception operations can be studied in FM 90-2: *Battlefield Deception* (Headquarters, Department of Army,Washington, DC, 3 October 1988). Its bibliography includes early Robert Jervis, Daniel Kahneman & Amos Tversky (prospect theory), and Roberta Wohlsetter.

assertive speech, body language, pressured pace, eye contact - designed to seize and hold the attention of the audience, as well as to gradually but inexorably replace their wills and judgment of reality with his own. [This is particularly essential to hypnotism. [95]]

c. **Dictation of the applicable elements.** The magician identifies to the audience what objects, locations, and/or procedures are important and essential, restricting the problem to their interaction exclusively. The consequence of this is that an object's behavior which might seem unremarkable or contrived against ordinary backgrounds or points of reference becomes surprising and inexplicable in this artificial environment.

d. **Definition of the variables.** An object or procedure may be used in any number of ways, but the magician defines them so as to limit these ways to only those which make possible and reinforce the illusion.

e. **Instruction of behavior.** Audience participation is desirable, since going through motions to supposedly produce the illusion suggests to the audience that it is somewhat responsible for it, thus encouraging belief in it.

f. **Limitation of possibilities.** As he controls all of the object(s) and procedure(s) variables, the magician can force the outcome of the illusion into one which the equally-predetermined alternatives appear to highlight as miraculous.

g. **Channeling of expectations.** Once in control of both the elements of the illusion and the audience's perceptions and willpower, the magician instructs the

---

[95] Cf. PSYCON #9.

audience in what the possible outcomes of the illusion can be. It is now "impossible" for the objects or procedures to function in any other way, nor for the audience to devise or consider one.

h. **Interpretation of the result.** Once the illusion is produced, the magician makes it clear to the audience what it "obviously" signifies. As in his initial establishment of control over the audience, he now implants - though announcement, emotional surprise/ satisfaction, and body language - their presumedly "spontaneous" reaction.

i. **Reinforcement of controlled perceptions.** As necessary to establish the performed illusion firmly in "reality", the magician follows it up with as many supporting devices and created impressions as are necessary.

Beyond these basics MW is most specifically concerned with the magical discipline of **mentalism**.[96] This involves diversion of target audience perceptions and interpretations towards a different interpretation of their own thought processes than the one which they would naturally experience. This is accomplished both through the above-listed techniques of magic and appropriate activation and blending of the previous eleven SLIMC PSYCONs. Every possible external and psychological factor is controlled and administered to not only reconfigure the subject's thought-processes, but to leave undisturbed his belief that absolutely no such external influence is occurring. Obviously, suspicion of or alertness to "mind control" can alarm or panic an

---

[96] Not to be confused with the clinical psychological or philosophical definitions of "mentalism".

individual, even if the activity is [as the Laws of MW require] completely ethical and benign.

The principles of mentalism may be studied in the literature of professional magic, and its power may be both experienced and applied in reputable institutions devoted to the art.[97] While mentalism is never used within MW operational activities to influence any of its planners or operatives, it permeates the entire manifestation of a MW campaign within the problem environment and to all non-MW onlookers. The original problem, if unsolvable, gradually and inconspicuously becomes one which is. Enemies are transformed into friends and allies. Apparently-rigid deadlines become unfolding options. Borders become gateways. Hoarded assets become horns of plenty. Overall, problems become opportunities, and hatred becomes affection, tolerance, and compassion.

MindWar is magic. Every MindWarrior must therefore be a magician.

13. PSYCON #13: Religion

a. The Phenomenon of Religion

Primitive pre-literate, pre-scientific humanity found itself a conscious actor within a bewilderingly complex and mysterious environment. The Earth obviously existed as it was perceived and experienced, but it did not "explain itself": Why natural objects and processes "are as they are" was [and still is] unknown, although both "pattern thinking" and the eventual onset of the "scientific method" at least enabled their substance,

---

97 Such as the Academy of Magical Arts of Hollywood, California:
http://www.magiccastle.com/
and the Magic Circle of the United Kingdom:
http://www.themagiccircle.co.uk/

properties, and behavior to be recognizable and predictable.

To address the "why", humans could only fall back upon their imagination, creating one or more "G/god[s]" and accompanying creation-myths. As humanity evolved, this practice branched into two general directions: metaphysics and religion.

(1) Metaphysics inspired the human intellect beyond the physical-sensory syllogisms of the natural universe into a realm of suprarational abstractions: the *neteru* of ancient Egypt, the Pythagorean/Platonic Forms. These principles were not identifiable through logic or reason, but through enlightened apprehension: what Plato referred to as *nœsis*. Cooperatively such awareness was obtained through rigorous schools of initiation.[98]

(2) The vast majority of humans, however, are incapable and/or unwilling to pursue or endure metaphysics. Hence they either live their lives ignoring the "why" question, or they accept any one of several modern-day continuations of the original, primitive superstitions: religion.

Within religions the "why" is simply assigned to the whim of one or more "gods", hence inexplicable. However it was, and remains, exploitable by persons and organizations wishing to control others by claiming to represent or interpret these gods/God images. The propaganda is simple: reward for obedience, punishment for disobedience - both in organic life and in a promised/ threatened hereafter. Such exploiters feel no obligation to explain or justify their actions; the masses are expected to take them on trust alone, or in the vernacular "faith". As Robert Anton Wilson quips: "Theology was a system for explaining things by coining words which nobody could

---

[98] These topics are addressed in my book *MindStar*.

understand and pretending that the words meant something."[99]

Religions invariably represent themselves as "forces for good" within the community, but the worldwide historical record shows quite the contrary: that they have consistently been invoked and exploited for destructive excesses: war, genocide, torture, and enslavement. This was most blatant during the "Dark Age" from the Christian Roman Empire and the Crusades to the 17th Century. After 1550 tensions between Catholics and Protestants had reached the stage of religious warfare, culminating in the terrible Thirty Years' War between Denmark, Sweden, and the Protestant German principalities on one hand and the Catholic Hapsburgs (Spain, Austria, Netherlands, Italy, and most of Catholic Germany) on the other. France, though Catholic, fought against the Hapsburgs for secular political reasons. Approximately one-third of Germany's population died from the war, and the final Peace of Westphalia (1648) was brought about more by exhaustion than by genuine reconciliation.

The subsequent Enlightenment and "Age of Reason" resulted as much from popular revulsion over such horrors as from the appearance of the functionally-atheistic "social contract" political theorists: Thomas Hobbes, John Locke, Jean-Jacques Rousseau, et al.

Since then - and this is a crucial realization for the MWarrior - religion in the Judæo/Christian West has become mere PSYOP by the power-elites, with no one except the uneducated masses taking it either literally or seriously. Ritualistic piety abounds; practical compliance with it is irrelevant.

---

[99] Robert Anton Wilson, *Schrödinger's Cat*. New York: Pocket Books, 1979, page #98.

b. Internal Religious PSYOP:
The Army Chaplain Corps

Our Father in Heaven, before we go into battle, every soldier among us will approach you each in his own way. Our enemies too, according to their own understanding, will ask for protection and for victory. And so we bow before your infinite wisdom. We offer our prayers as best we can. I pray you watch over the young Jack Geoghegan that I lead into battle. You use me as your instrument in this awful hell of war to watch over them. Especially if they're men like this one beside me, deserving of a future in your blessing and goodwill. Amen.

Oh, yes, and one more thing, dear Lord, about our enemies, ignore their heathen prayers and help us blow those little bastards straight to Hell. Amen.

    - Lt. Colonel Hal Moore
     [in the post chapel before leaving for Vietnam]
     We Were Soldiers (2002)

Although *pro forma* the mission of the Army Chaplain Corps is "to advise commanders concerning soldiers' free exercise of religion"[100], in practice it has a fourfold *de facto* mission: (1) to convince soldiers that their religious faith should not stand in the way of killing other humans on order; (2) to reassure soldiers that God is on their side in a war, even if it is against other humans professing faith in the same God; (3) through these first two missions to minimize or dispel soldiers' fear of death in combat; and (4) to ensure that soldiers' families do not compromise the first three missions.

To reinforce this agenda, chaplains are commissioned as uniformed officers and are dependent for both retention and promotion on their secular commanders' evaluations. Those who find they cannot reconcile combat missions and orders with their faiths either resign or are removed.

---

[100] https://www.army.mil/chaplaincorps#org-about

These facts are not mentioned to gratuitously embarrass the Chaplain Corps, but rather to simply acknowledge its critical PW function. Doctrinally Judæo/Christian religions prohibit the killing of humans who have done nothing to deserve it, and for the PW U.S. Army to function, it must order, and rely upon its soldiers to carry out such orders: the individual- and mass-killing of government-declared "enemies".

After World War II much sanctimonious publicity was given the so-called "Nürnberg Principle": that soldiers could not use "obedience to orders" to justify destructive actions which others might later label "war crimes". This "Principle" was applied exclusively to the vanquished Axis, however, and others have since never regarded it as a valid objection by individual soldiers.[101]

The result of this official/institutional hypocrisy is a cancerous erosion of the U.S. Army's honor and integrity, which, because of this nation's original and traditional stand on behalf of individual ethics, are absolutely indispensable to it.

Once the American armed forces evolve from PW to MW, the arbitrary killing of "enemies" will cease, and the need for chaplains' PSYOP of service personnel will evaporate. The implied-coercive commissioned Chaplain Corps will be discontinued, to be replaced by civilian clergy with no PW-enforcement agenda.

c. Application of the MW PSYCON

Once the U.S. Army has removed its own religion-blinders as discussed above, it will be in a position to objectively and accurately use the Religion PSYCON in MW campaigns.

---

[101] Cf. *Law of* [PW] *War* above in this chapter.

As historically, religion remains today a powerful force in the motivating of humans to PW violence. As this book goes to press in 2016, America's politically-pronounced "enemy" of convenience is Judæo/Christianity's principal competitor, Islam. [It is the most transparent of protests that this enemy is only "bad" Islam.]

Historically this new "enemy" was needed, and chosen, when the Soviet Union and its Warsaw Pact allies collapsed and "Communism" was no longer plausible as a masses-inflaming threat. [To test this, simply look for any mention of "Islamic Terrorism" prior to the fall of the Berlin Wall in 1989; there is none.]

As has been made clear in this book, MW does not permit "sacrificial lambs" under any guise. Humans are regarded and respected as humans, regardless of their nationality, ethnicity, religion, or any other arbitrary qualifier.

The first step in the application of the "Religion PSYCON", therefore, is to remove "religion" as an "enemy". As with MW generally, the enemy is never "other humans" in any arbitrary classification; it is the overall "problem of conflict" in which all involved/affected humans cooperate to resolve by *áristos*.

Next it is merely needed to recall that all institutional religions are nothing more than masses-control devices by their respective power-elites, and that the motives and goals of those elites are not in the least "spiritual" but material. In short, they seek power in terms of money, sovereign territory, and enough of an indoctrinated population-base to appear a credible future PW threat to any challenger.

Once identified, these PW motives can be removed by fulfilling them within a mutually-cooperative balance. If international recognition of occupied territory is sought, grant it. If trade is sought, allow it. In short, go down the list of tensions for which "religion" is being used as a PW defense mechanism and remove them openly, cooperatively, and rationally - without any reference whatever to "religion". Once these actual, secular problems are resolved, "religion" will disappear by itself into its non-PW role as just one of many community-control ideologies.

14. PSYCON #14: Sex

> Alice Harford: Millions of years of evolution, right? Right? Men have to stick it in every place they can, but for women ... women it is just about security and commitment and whatever the fuck else!
> Dr. Bill Harford: A little oversimplified, Alice, but yes, something like that.
> Alice Harford: If you men only knew!
> *- Eyes Wide Shut* (1999)

Organic life on Earth is divided into two complementary functions, conventionally called "male" and "female" or collectively "sex". Why this should be so is one of the mysteries of nature, although its apparent result is the preservation and strengthening of a species by facilitating reproduction by the strongest of each gender.

On the male side, males compete with and eliminate other males for the right to capture, control, and reproduce through the strongest and most desirable females.

On the female side, females compete amongst themselves for access to the strongest, most powerful, most desirable males, in order to be captured by them and reproduce by them. As with males, this may involve eliminating other females.

Weaker members of both sexes may also survive, pair, and breed, within the tolerance of the stronger pairs.

Alternately they may not pair or breed, but become drones of work- but not reproduction-significance.

Over this natural simplicity human communities have thrown various overlays of convention in order to survive and function cooperatively, eventually as states, ultimately as nations. The earliest such overlay was religion (cf. PSYCON #13), which excused and justified male capture and control of females as a God-dictated patriarchy. Men no longer needed to feel oppressive; women were expected to accept subordination and obedience. The resulting patriarchy was characteristic of the entire civilized world of antiquity, with the notable exception of Egypt and Minoan Crete as gender-equal cultures.

This institution of patriarchy has continued through history to the present, where only in the most recent centuries, and then only in a relatively few more post-Enlightenment, Age of Reason-impacted societies has it begun to be dismantled at least in part. In areas such as North America and Western Europe today, women are nominally equal under the law, can vote, own property, etc.

But it is far from a return to ancient Egypt or Crete. Men still feel a right to control women, and an expectation that "true" women need and want to be so controlled. [The endless arguments over abortion decision are a case in point.] Women are correspondingly uncertain whether absolute independence and equality are "authentically womanly" or a metamorphosis into a sexless drone-state. Individual disparities in class, wealth, and power exacerbate such confusion for both sexes. The tension and frustration have also given rise to "escapes" such as homosexuality and attempts to "transgender" through cross-dressing and hormone/surgery self-mutilation.

This is a tragic and pathetically inept response to nature's harsh regimen of competitive heterosexuality. Its net effect is ludicrous confusion over sexual roles and maturity in the "emancipated" cultures, while the [much larger] rest of the planet continues to perpetuate religion-justified patriarchy, often to extremes of callousness and cruelty.

MindWar does not propose to resolve America's sexual turmoil, much less anyone else's. As Alice Harford observed, it is a contest ultimately between millions of years of natural evolution vs. clumsy rationality.

This PSYCON is identified rather to note that many, indeed most of the world's PW-prone societies remain very much in the grip of centuries-old religious patriarchies. This characteristic, along with such societies' antipathy towards the United States for its perceived "sexual degeneracy", must be factored into any MW campaign as non-confrontationally as possible. The U.S. should not expect other countries or cultures to align to its sexual climate, and vice-versa. *Áristos* here is best sought through solutions and compromises that are sexual/gender non-specific.

Chapter 4: MetaForce Branch[102]
[Formerly: Special Forces Branch]

---

[102] The MetaForce Branch (MFB) insignia replaces the old Special Forces Branch:

The crossed arrows of gold date back to the First Special Service Force of World War II, and have been traditionally continued through the Special Forces era. In MFB they are shown in gold, no longer alternating silver, establishing that MF is finally and formally a Branch of the Army. The tips of the arrows end in lightning bolts, not arrowheads, signifying that MF targets the mind, not the body. Over the arrows rises the traditional Special Forces dagger, with its black-wrapped handle and black hilt. Its blade, however, is now green flame, honoring the Green Beret and signifying that it is an instrument of metaphysical illumination, not a weapon for killing.

The term "Special Forces" (which signifies only "other" and "plural") is superseded by "MetaForce": literally "the force that is beyond force".

The MFB color is Beret Green.

The old "Special Forces Tab" is discontinued [since, among other things, it is no longer suited to the Army dress uniform]. As only MF-qualified soldiers are admitted to the Branch, the MFB insignia alone indicates MF qualification; there is no separate badge or tab.

The incorrect-Latin motto *De Oppresso Liber* is corrected to *De Oppressione Liberare*.

MFB unit members wear the green beret with all uniforms except the dress blue.

The Green Beret is again becoming a symbol of excellence, a badge of courage, a mark of distinction in the fight for freedom. I know the United States Army will live up to its reputation for imagination, resourcefulness, and spirit as we meet this challenge.

- John F. Kennedy (1962)

He who fights monsters must beware lest in doing so he does not become a monster. And if you gaze long into the Abyss, the Abyss also gazes into you.

- Friedrich Nietzsche
Beyond Good and Evil (1886)

A. Original Concept

The classical image of war is that of two national, uniformed armies, together with their similarly-national, uniformed allied armies, contesting one another on the battlefield in compartmentalized, set-piece engagements. Civilians and communities are not involved, except where battles or troop movements incidentally, accidentally, temporarily spill over into them.

This of course has certainly not been the case since the two World Wars, and indeed not generally before them either. People who aren't soldiers in national armies, who don't wear uniforms, sometimes get frightened, angry, or just principled enough to pick up a gun, brick, or stone and attack their perceived oppressors.[103] Throughout history such persons or groups have been known by many names, such as

---

[103] "On the radio talk shows and TV, you hear one thing again and again: how the U.S.A. stands for freedom, and we come to the aid of a friend. But who are the ones we call our friends - these governments killing their own? Or the people who finally can't take any more, and pick up a gun or a brick or a stone? There are lives in the balance; there are people under fire; there are children at the cannons; and there is blood on the wire." - Jackson Browne, *Lives in the Balance* (1986)

"irregulars", "partisans", and "guerrillas". Governments call them "patriots" or "freedom fighters" if they approve of them, and "terrorists" or "insurgents" if they don't.

In World War II the United States sought to ally itself with, and control, anti-Axis patriots and freedom fighters through the Office of Strategic Services (OSS), which would develop into the postwar Central Intelligence Agency (CIA).

Simultaneously the U.S. and Canadian Armies experimented with the binational 1st Special Service Force as a combat brigade (the "Devil's Brigade" or "Black Devils") capable of parachuting behind enemy lines and conducting assault operations in adverse weather. While this unit is traditionally regarded as the predecessor of the U.S. Army's Special Forces (SF), its mission more closely resembles that of Ranger units.

When SF was established in 1952, its original function was unconventional warfare (UW), being the training and support of guerrilla forces in an enemy nation or its occupied countries, the obvious scenario being a Warsaw Pact-overrun Western Europe.[104] When a Warsaw Pact attack did not materialize, and when instead the U.S. found itself supporting regimes, including extremely repressive ones, that were grappling with communist movements, SF's function changed to the defeat, not support of UW. The new mission statements were foreign internal defense (FID) and counterinsurgency [later counterterrorism]. The teaching and training function of

---

[104] "At this time (1952-55) this true 'Post Strike' role of SF was TOP SECRET and very closely held. They would go into the enemy area not only for tactical reasons, but because they were trained by the WW2 Civil Affairs & Military Government (CAMG) specialists to help friendly natives reorganize the Soviet government. It was presumed that after a nuclear strike much of the government, communications, transportation, and other infrastructural elements would be decimated." - Letter, L.F. Prouty to M. Aquino 7/2/95.

SF also changed to include special reconnaissance (SR) and direct action (DA), exemplified by MACV-SOG during the Vietnam War. From John Wayne's personification of the "Green Berets" as warm-hearted, well-intentioned samaritans in his 1968 movie of the same name, SF's image gradually changed to that of the lone-wolf supercommando portrayed by Sylvester Stallone in his *Rambo* series of action films.

This Jekyll/Hyde odyssey has left today's SF in something of an identity crisis. It believes it exists "to free the oppressed" [per its famous motto *De Oppresso Liber*[105]], yet in the PW universe it more often than not finds itself in locations, with assignments, whose goal is that of repressing domestic rebellion, regardless of local popular or moral motives.

B. General Y and Colonel X

The postwar identity of SF was conceived and implemented significantly by two U.S. Air Force officers, Major General Edward W. Lansdale (1908-1987) and Colonel L. Fletcher Prouty (1917-2001).[106]   Lansdale became a UW legend and "man of mystery" during the 1950-53 Huk rebellion in the Philippines, which he significantly helped the Magsaysay government thwart through a creative propaganda campaign blending an active empathy for the populace's perceived problems

---

[105] In correct Latin this would be *De Oppressione Liberare*, but like "Git thar fustest with the mostest." (a misquotation of Lt. General Nathan Bedford Forrest, CSA), the mistranslation has immortalized itself in tradition.

[106] Lansdale and Prouty would later be portrayed as "General Y" and [Colonel] "X" in Oliver Stone's 1991 film *JFK*.

with an underlying and ultimately governing commitment to U.S. strategic interests.[107]

In March 1954 the National Security Council published document #5412 defining U.S. covert operations, placing the CIA in charge with DOD providing personnel, base, and logistical support. All such operations were to be "plausibly deniable" and no active duty military personnel were to be involved in them.[108]

That same year CIA Director Allen Dulles created the Saigon Military Mission (which was CIA, not DOD) and assigned Lansdale to head it.[109] Lansdale moved to South Vietnam, wherein he attempted a similar defeat of the National Liberation Front (aka "Viet Cong") on behalf of the Diem government. Here, through continuing to be media-glamorized,[110] he was not so successful, since the regime was dealing not with an indigenous movement but one deriving from and actively controlled by North Vietnam.

The 1963 downfall of the regime and subsequent introduction of American combat forces effectively eclipsed Lansdale's efforts in that conflict, although President Johnson would later send him briefly back.

---

[107] Jonathan Nashel, *Edward Lansdale's Cold War.* Amherst: University of Massachusetts Press, 2005, pages #138-9.

[108] "This is the real reason why the so-called 'air support' myth got started after the Bay of Pigs. Everyone knew beforehand that no active duty military personnel could become involved. It had nothing to do with a JFK decision. McGeorge Bundy called off the JFK-directed air strike on D-Day, and that is what caused the failure." - Letter, L.F. Prouty to M. Aquino 7/2/95.

[109] *Ibid.*

[110] Lansdale was caricatured first in Graham Greene's 1955 novel *The Quiet American*, then in William Lederer & Eugene Burdick's 1958 response *The Ugly American*, both made into major Hollywood films.

Prouty's UW involvement began in 1955, when, as the USAF's first Chief of Special Operations, he was both its liaison to the CIA's MKULTRA and the creator of its global CIA operational USAF support system.[111] In 1960 he was assigned to the Office of the Secretary of Defense where [under first Gates, then McNamara] he served in the same capacity for all the services. Simultaneously Lansdale had become the liaison between OSD and CIA. As Prouty recalls:

> Lansdale saw an opportunity to expand this combined tactical role even more. He planned to bring the SF, the CIA, and the CAMG people all together. He went down to talk with some friends at the Department of the Army, but the climate was not right and Ed could not get things going. It appeared that the Army did not much care for Special Warfare.
>
> This didn't stop him, and he broadened his contacts to include the old Continental Army Command (CONARC), which supervised the CAMG School and provided him with its curriculum. This he divided among the three of us (Lansdale, Prouty, and Sam Wilson - Wilson was a veteran of the WW2 Merrill's Marauders). The result was the new SF curriculum at Fort Bragg in 1960, following the JFK election but prior to his inauguration. By the time the SF School began these classes in late 1960, a number of the key officers and instructors were actually CIA under military cover. I was there for the first classes just to see how things worked out. When it was ready for a formal commencement, Deputy SecDef James Douglas did the honors. This is how the Special Warfare concepts were put in motion and how the "Green Berets" got their send-off - and got removed from the "Post Strike" role. It was not a JFK deal in any way until 1961, and then only inferentially.[112]

---

[111] Letter, Prouty to Aquino 5/12/95. In MKULTRA Prouty worked primarily with Ewen Cameron, Louis Jolyon "Jolly" West, and Jim Monroe.

[112] Letter, Prouty to Aquino 7/2/95.

Following JFK's 1961 inauguration Lansdale was summoned to the White House to brief the new President on the Vietnam situation, and returned to tell Prouty "I believe I have a chance for the Ambassadorship." [113] After the Bay of Pigs disaster, however, the CIA was *non grata* in the Administration, and Lansdale's hopes were dashed. [114] He was relegated to running the CIA's MONGOOSE operation against Cuba, and only after the JFK assassination did the next President Lyndon Johnson reassign him to Vietnam 1965-7. But by then the Vietnam War had escalated beyond Lansdale's possible control. [115]

C. Vietnam: Heart of Darkness

Upon arrival of U.S. combat forces in South Vietnam, SF was relegated to working with the Montagnards and other non-Vietnamese ethnic groups in the more remote areas of the country, and to conducting clandestine combat, rescue, and cross-border operations under the

---

[113] *Ibid.*

[114] Lansdale, according to Prouty, executed the JFK assassination with MONGOOSE assets. "He had hundreds of trained and skilled men whom he could use to flesh out the cover story that the true decision-makers had to have to protect the real hit team, and create the three decades of cover story that has embarrassed American citizens since that date. Without such a cover story the murder and resultant *coup d'etat* could not have been achieved so effectively. JFK would not give him that Ambassadorship for which he would have killed. What else could he do?" - *Ibid.*

[115] "I put Lansdale over there but nothing happened." - Lyndon Johnson to Drew Pearson, *Washington Post*, 7/11/66.

auspices of MACV-SOG.[116]   That SF acquitted itself with great distinction in both responsibilities is beyond question.[117] In the process, however, it drew further away from Lansdale's original vision of a trifunctional PSYOP/ SF/CA task force.

By the time of the Iraq and Afghanistan invasions, SF had become essentially an extension of the conventional Army's occupation presence into areas too remote and inaccessible for conventional units. SF's "commando" role predominates, with efforts to encourage cooperation by local inhabitants continued as possible. What eludes this posture, however, is a solution to the underlying sociopolitical discontents and imbalances that flow in to regain control of an area whenever SF is not physically present. Thus as with other PW assets, SF has become a treater of the symptoms, not the disease.

D. Evolution to MetaForce Branch

The evolution of Army Special Forces into MetaForce Branch (MFB) transforms both the way the resource is

---

[116] SF's decline in prestige was further dramatized by the harsh official action taken against 5th Group Commander Colonel Robert Rheault and members of his command in 1969 for the killing of a Vietnamese double-agent. The Secretary of the Army dismissed the murder and conspiracy charges when both the CIA and MACV Commanding General Creighton Abrams refused to testify. The incident inspired Francis Ford Coppola's 1979 film *Apocalypse Now*, in which he modeled the Marlon Brando character of Colonel Kurtz on Rheault. Cf. Peter Cowie, *The Apocalypse Now Book* (Da Capo Press, 2000).

[117] The 5th Special Forces Group was awarded the Presidential Unit Citation (Army) Vietnam 1966-1968, Meritorious Unit Commendation (Army) Vietnam 1968; Republic of Vietnam Cross of Gallantry with Palm, Vietnam 1964-1969; Republic of Vietnam Civil Action Honor Medal, 1st Class, Vietnam 1968-1970. During the Vietnam War, seventeen Medals of Honor were awarded to its soldiers.

internally organized and the way it is applied in future MW campaigns. In essence MFB becomes the physical presence of the entire MW campaign in the situation-area, both before the campaign formally commences and until its condition sufficiently stabilizes to permit MFB's replacement by the ParaPolitics (PP) Branch teams.

As with the MW campaign overall, MFB's mission is to identify, diagnose, and constructively treat the destabilizing "disease" itself, not its symptoms [of local killing and destruction].

While MFB teams are armed, such weapons are both designed and intended only for team protection and that of other humans in instances where all other MW devices have failed. They are a "last resort" and an indicator of MW failure, and are always regarded as such. They are thus always concealed on MFB soldiers' persons - never openly displayed. They are produced only when it is unavoidably necessary to use them, and then only to a necessary minimum.

Here it is essential to recall that it is the function of the MWB to so research, comprehend, and precondition a situation area that when MF teams actually touch down, they will encounter only non-stressed, receptive, and positively-disposed inhabitants. At no time will MFB teams be deployed to an area which has not been successfully MW-preconditioned.

E. Precedents and Principles

1. Shaolin *Kung Fu*

For most people the term *kung fu* brings to mind dramatic unarmed combat by highly-skilled, intensively-disciplined Chinese martial artists [as well as non-Chinese enthusiasts]. This is a misapprehension and oversimplification. The term *kung fu* translates to "to know what to do", and it is most properly understood as an entire way of life: a constant harmonizing of oneself with one's surroundings and the correction of anything inharmonious to its ideal alignment.

Traditionally *kung fu* dates to the 6th century C.E., when the Indian Buddhist monk Bodhidharma journeyed to the Shaolin Taoist monastery of China and taught the monks a form of active meditative dancing. Over the subsequent centuries this developed into the famous system of acrobatic self-defense.

The Taoist and Buddhist roots of the Shaolin discipline, however, are both integral with it and essential to it. Taoism, originated ca. the 5th-6th centuries B.C.E. by Lao Tzu, comprises both the apprehension of the singularity of nature and the quest for conscious melding with it.[118] Buddhism, originating in India in the same approximate time-period, generally prescribes a path to personal enlightenment through a moderate, monastic lifestyle. Consequently *kung fu* became an active expression of these combined philosophies.

The MFB soldier is not expected to be either a Taoist or a Buddhist. What is required of him is a *kung fu* sensitivity to imbalances in situations to which he is sent, and "knowing what to do" to resolve them.

2. *Ch'i*

Another concept from ancient China is that of *ch'i* [or *qi*], the "life force" of each living being.[119]   It is the presence of *ch'i* which distinguished a living body from a

---

[118]   *Tao* is usually translated as "the Way" [in the sense of the onflowing of the natural universe]. It is most closely reflected in the classic *Tao Te Ching*, authored by Lao Tzu.

[119]   *Ch'i* was originally and extensively discussed in *The Yellow Emperor's Classic of Internal Medicine*, 27/2600 BCE.

dead one, and which links the physical mechanism with the metaphysical soul. Consequently the strength and concentration of the will are conveyed to the physical senses and structures through *ch'i*, while diminished or disrupted *ch'i* results in confusion and exhaustion.

Until the late 20th century, Western science tended to dismiss *ch'i* as a folk myth, since it supposedly could not be detected or measured in the laboratory. What has since transpired is that it was indeed there all along, and completely detectable: It is simply the body's complete and component EMFs.

All physical energy, no matter how it is generated [or, more precisely, converted] is a function of the electromagnetic spectrum (EMS). The human mental processes which command a muscular action, for instance, transmit that command by electrical impulses to that muscle, and the EMS waves or disruptions subsequently detected by the visual, auditory, and tactile receptors signal the accuracy and effectiveness of the action. *Ch'i* is thus a measurement of the strength and accuracy of such activity, both deliberately and in the body's unconscious functions [as in the heartbeat, digestion, and breathing].

The smooth flow of *ch'i* is enhanced, reasonably enough, through proper care of the mind and body: diet, rest, breathing, exercise, and mental coherence. Conscious mental/physical conditioning exercises are known as *ch'i kung* [or *qi gong*] (= *ch'i* coherence"). While a systematic discipline of *ch'i kung* is the ideal way to maintain strong and harmonious bodily *ch'i*, Chinese medicine also proposed to treat specific disruptions of its circulation through the placement of special needles (acupuncture) or massage pressure (*shiatsu*).

Less positively, *t'ai chi ch'uan* martial artists defeat opponents by strikes precisely targeted to disrupt their *ch'i* flow and coherence. *T'ai chi ch'uan*, literally "supreme ultimate boxing" is better known in the contemporary West as a smooth-flowing exercise program rather than a combat technique. Indeed, because the *ch'i*-directed strikes of *t'ai chi ch'uan* practitioners could, for that very reason, be severely harmful or lethal, they are generally forbidden in martial arts sport competitions.

As discussed in Chapter #3 under "G.5. PSYCON #4: Chronobiology", the human body and mind are strongly influenced by external natural cycles, including the geomagnetic field of the Earth. Subtle variations in this field, known as the "Schumann Resonances (SR)", are detected by magnetically-sensitive particles (magnetite) in the pineal gland of the brain, which regulates the circadian cycle by the generation and release of Melatonin.[120]

The SR consist of an EMS field between the Earth and the ionosphere, pulsing at between 7-10 Hz. This tends to entrain humans to *alpha* (8-14 Hz) BWR, especially during periods of strong, higher-range SR, associated with daylight and atmospheric lightning activity. This is obviously MW campaign-helpful. At night the ionosphere moves higher, resulting in a decrease of the SR towards its lower 7 Hz extreme. This entrains *theta* BWR, hence altered states of consciousness and similarly-unusual moods and behavior: **not** MW campaign-helpful.

Through the detection and calculation of SR, or what the Chinese termed "external *ch'i*", it may be possible to predetermine circadian mental and physical states of those in MW-campaign areas.

In addition to the detection and prediction of externally-influenced *ch'i*, it is theoretically possible [and asserted by advanced *ch'i* martial artists] to first

---

[120] Cf. George J. Washnis & R.Z. Hricak, *Discovery of Magnetic Health*. Rockville, MD: Nova Publishing Company, 1993.

consciously regulate one's own *ch'i* [e.g. through meditation reduce one's BWR to *theta*] for extreme powers of concentration, then project an even lower BWR of *delta* (1-4 Hz) into an opponent, thus rendering him dazed or unconscious.[121] The *delta* BWR is concentrated by the sender in his hands, then extended as an EMF into the opponent, entraining first his pineal gland, then through it his brain's internal BWR pacemaker, the thalamus.[122] Its thalamocortical neurons experience a "silent phase" every 1-25 seconds, during which time they are susceptible to such external entrainment.[123]

This "mirror neuron" effect, in which the firing of a particular neuron in one individual's brain triggers a similar firing in another's, is commonly experienced by and familiar to recipients as intuition of the originator's emotions, attitude, or intentions; when someone else picks up a knife, for instance, one senses whether this is or is not a prelude to violence with it. This normally unconscious, passive phenomenon is employed actively and deliberately by the MFB soldier to change both the perceptions and the anticipations of those on whom he is

---

[121] Cf. David Eisenberg & Thomas Lee Wright, *Encounters with Qi: Exploring Chinese Medicine.* New York: W.W. Norton, 1995. In Japanese Ninjutsu this technique is referred to as *ki ken* (the "spirit fist").

[122] The projection is simply the controlled EMF of the sender, which extends sufficiently beyond his body to envelop and entrain the receptive/ uncontrolled BWR of the opponent. Cf. James L. Oschman, *Energy Medicine: The Scientific Basis.* New York: Churchhill Livingstone, 2000.

[123] Cf. Andersen, Per & Andersson, Sven Anders, *Physiological Basis of the Alpha Rhythm.* New York: Appleton-Century Crofts, 1968.

concentrating [whereupon they will look for other droids[124]].[125]

Summarily the MFB soldier encountering groups or individuals in a MW campaign locale, may augment preconditioning MWB PSYCONs by calculating the influence of external natural EMF/*ch'i*, and by self-conditioning and then projecting a calming, positive, or if necessary gently incapacitating personal EMF.[126]

3. Negotiation

So let us not be blind to our differences - but let us also direct attention to our common interests and the means by which those differences can be resolved. And if we cannot end now our differences, at least we can help make the world safe for diversity. For, in the final analysis, our most basic common link is that we all inhabit this small planet. We all breathe the same air. We all cherish our children's futures. And we are all mortal.

- John F. Kennedy[127]

Once a receptive and cooperative atmosphere has been established, the MFB team proceeds to implement the *áristos*. If possible this is effected by straightforward reasoning and convincing, for which there are many conventional recipes.

---

[124] Cf. Chapter 4, PSYCON #12: Magic.

[125] Cf. Marco Iacoboni, Roger P. Woods, Marcel Brass, Harold Bekkering, John C. Mazziotta, Giacomo Rizzolatti, "Cortical Mechanisms of Human Imitation", *Science* Magazine, December 24, 1999, pages #2526-8.

[126] The reader may have experienced situations in which merely the arrival and presence of a particular individual exerts a calming, cooperative influence upon those present. This is a scientific explanation for such encounters and experiences.

[127] Commencement address, American University, June 10, 1963

a. Negotiation Procedure

Here it must be emphasized that what is being applied is not just casual, amateur discussion [which in tenuous situations can and frequently does collapse into emotional grandstanding]. Rather it is a disciplined, calculated process based not just upon rational reasoning, but also upon every other factor (emotion, religion, ideology, ethnicity, culture, economics, etc.) which frames and constrains the issue. **The MFB team will be pre-practiced in this before it ever touches down.**

As developed in the classic primer of negotiation technique *Getting to Yes*, negotiation is not waded into haphazardly.[128] Rather it is carefully structured and executed to reach constructive closure:

(1) As with MW generally, the people involved are removed from being the "problem" [or "enemy"]; the problem [or MW "enemy"] is redefined as the situational issues over which there is disagreement and friction.

(2) Initially each participant in a disagreement is identified and defined in terms of a **position** taken and articulated, which tends to an oversimplified caricature of the situation and the belief that it cannot be changed. Hence such

---

[128] Cf. Roger Fisher, William L. Ury, & Bruce Patton, *Getting to Yes: Negotiating Agreement Without Giving In*. New York: Penguin Books, 1983 *et seq.*, - and in obstinate cases Ury's supplementary *Getting Past No: Negotiating in Difficult Situations*. New York: Bantam Books, 1993. Fisher & Ury's approach became codified as the Harvard Project on Negotiation. Another influential, alternative approach is Max Bazerman's work at Harvard Business School, which relates to Kahneman & Tversky's prospect theory, and to Cass Sunstein and Richard Thaler's behavioral economics work.

positions are not discussed; rather the problem is recontextualized in terms of the participants' individual and collective **interests**: with the problem being a/the impediment to their fulfillment. Here commonality of all participants' interests is sought and emphasized, lending momentum to solutions which will benefit all rather than just one or some participants.

(3)   Initial disagreements polarize when the issues are condensed into simplistic, either/or lines-drawn. The problem must accordingly be diffused into a complex of flexible variables, each of which can be addressed and adjusted without triggering intransigence in any participant. As each of the component variables is adjusted with an eye to the greatest collective benefit, so the entire matrix will move towards that *áristos*.

(4)   Not only the commonality of the problem, but the worth and dignity of all participants involved must permeate the negotiation. Hatred or contempt towards other participants, if sensed [and as is easy to sense], will nullify any attempt at reasoned discussion. [129]

b. Physiological Considerations[130]

Crucial to negotiation - indeed to the entire concept of MW - is the presumption of orderliness in the human

---

[129] This reflects the overwhelming of algorithmic by pattern thought, as discussed in Chapter 4.E.

[130]   This extremely pertinent and crucial factor was incisively introduced by Dr. William Henry Anderson in "Terrorism: The Underlying Causes", *The Intelligencer* (Washington, D.C.: Association of Former Intelligence Officers, Winter/Spring 2004).

thinking process. We assume that, whether logically, emotionally, or environmentally, the human brain processes impressions, information, and accumulated knowledge methodically and consequentially. This is the entire basis upon which human behavior can be comprehended and predicted, on both the individual and the group level.

The unspoken, and all too often ignored assumption in this scenario is that the brain is whole, healthy, and functioning perfectly. Unfortunately this is not always, and perhaps not even mostly the case.

The human brain, like other components of the body, requires essential care and insulation from harm from the moment of its prenatal origin if it is to develop and mature fully functional. This tends to be taken for granted in highly-developed countries, where good nutrition, medicine, and safety from environmental hazards (lead, mercury, pollution, etc.) are the norm.

In many areas of the world, however, expectant mothers and their subsequent children are malnourished and in peril of numerous diseases. Children may be subject to psychological and physiological hardship from the moment of birth. The outward effects of this can be seen in stunted growth, fragile health, impaired faculties. Not so evident is the condition and capacity of the individual's brain.

While the entire brain may suffer from such inadequacies and injuries, particularly pertinent to the discretionary behavioral process is an area called the **amygdala**. In concert with the judgment centers of the frontal cortex, it assigns significance and priority to information. If this process is impaired, the result can be distorted or disproportionate opinions or expressions. At minimum this may manifest as a harmless personal fixation. More ominously and extremely it can result in irrational and unchangeable fanaticism.

Fortunately extreme cases rarely wind up in political or social positions of authority; they are too conspicuously recognized by others as dangerous "loose cannons". Less fortunately, this is a sliding-scale phenomenon, where some degree of impairment may not be easily identifiable. Many of history's most infamous tyrants, from Caligula to Stalin, exhibited a streak of callousness and cruelty which blindsided those about them and confounded later biographers and historians.

Central to Plato's thought, and indeed to the premise of MW, is that no intelligent individual will deliberately choose, or do, evil. Rather it is intrinsic to human nature that we aspire to the Good, the *Agathon*.[131] When someone makes a decision or takes an action which is apparently evil, therefore, it is the result of either misperception of causal factors or, as noted here, impaired judgment faculties.

MFT negotiators, if and when they encounter nonsensical, untouchable fanaticism in confronted persons, obviously cannot undertake to be amateur brain surgeons [even if the amygdala were "adjustable"]. They will either have to overcome the resistance through applied PSYCONs or attempt to marginalize or remove the impeding personality.[132] Of the several PSYCONs discussed in Chapter #3, it is #12/Magic which is most immediately and easily employable in face-to-face impasses.

---

[131] See Chapter 5 for further discussion of the *Agathon*.

[132] This should **not** be taken to mean abduction or murder. Both easier and more productive are distraction or preemption of such a person's interest and attention, such that the actual problem of MW concern can be pursued with others.

4. Magic

In situations where all attempts at direct, rational convincing fail, the MFB team next resorts to magic. The essence of magic, as developed in Chapter #3 under "H. 12. PSYCON #12: Magic", is the manipulation of the perceptions of the other party so that he first redefines the problem and its issues for himself, then draws conclusions as to the reality and options available based on that redefinition. In short, if the ostensible problem appears to be unsolvable, change it into one which is. In creating such an alternative, the MFB magician unobtrusively introduces a scenario which addresses the actual problem without seeming to, and this is accomplished not by lying to or deceiving those involved, but by presenting them with impressions that lead them to such interpretations and conclusions by themselves.[133]

F. "A Spoonful of Sugar"

The function of MFB in a MW campaign is to stabilize the on-site situation sufficiently for the PPB to touch down and commence its reenvision of that situation, as discussed in the next chapter. Thus MFB is not an invasion or occupation entity, and if properly functioning will not be present long enough for the local populace to begin to perceive it as such. If it cannot accomplish its mission in a very short timespan, almost before those encountering it begin to focus on its presence, MWB has failed to adequately precondition the situation. In that case the MFB presence should be withdrawn until it is so preconditioned.

---

[133] Cf. Al Schneider, *The Theory and Practice of Magic Deception.* CreateSpace Independent Publishing Platform, 2011.

In action a MFB team is "invisible". Its members materialize without attracting notice, they work to adjust the situation without seeming to interfere with it, and finally they disappear just as unobtrusively as they arrived. The MFB model is not John Rambo; it is Mary Poppins.[134]

> Just a spoonful of sugar helps the medicine go down in the most delightful way. In every job that must be done, there is an element of fun. You find the fun, and - **snap** - the job's a game!
>
> - Mary Poppins

---

[134] Who is, appropriately, Airborne-qualified.

Chapter 5: ParaPolitics Branch[135]
[Formerly: Civil Affairs Branch]

> Until philosophers are kings, or the kings and princes of this
> world have the spirit and power of philosophy, and political
> greatness and wisdom meet in one, and those commoner
> natures who pursue either to the exclusion of the other are
> compelled to stand aside, cities will never have rest from
> their evils - no, nor the human race, as I believe - and then
> only will this our State have a possibility of life and behold
> the light of day.
>
> - Plato, *The Republic* (Book VI, 473-C

---

[135] The ParaPolitics Branch (PPB) insignia replaces the old Civil
Affairs Branch:

Against a globe of the Earth in sea-blue rises a torch whose Branch-
traditional purple base flows into a Mental Blue crown and the rose-
quartz flame of Illuminated wisdom. Diagonally secondarily dexter
across the torch is a Mental Blue sword ending in the MW lightning-
bolt. Diagonally primarily sinister is a parchment scroll inscribed
with the ancient Greek term καλοκαγαθία. As developed by Plato in
the *Gorgias*, *kalokagathia* identifies "moral virtue reflecting both the
natural and the conventional": the key to both individual and
community perfection. The PPB colors continue from Civil Affairs as
purple and white. PPB unit members wear the purple beret with all
uniforms except the dress blue.

A. Original Concept

The need for armies to do something about the human suffering and landed wreckage they left behind them in PhysWar is as old as PhysWar itself. Doing nothing meant increased, prolonged misery and engendering of hatreds that would eventually give rise to new, angrier enemies and wars. Sometimes, as in the case of Troy or Carthage, the victor's solution was to completely obliterate the vanquished, so that there would be nothing **to** reemerge from its ashes. But as the object of most PWs was conquest and acquisition of human and territorial assets, such a solution was increasingly impractical.

It was the Romans who most famously recognized the need to make allies of those they conquered, granting Roman citizenship generously throughout their empire and extending such benefits as the construction of roads and waterways, and the preservation of social order by Roman garrisons as well. The result was the *Pax Romana* and a confluence of cultures unprecedented in the ancient world [though previously attempted, but not sustained, by Alexander the Great].

Until World War II the assets used by the U.S. Army for such postbattle cleanup work were hastily and awkwardly thrown together, then abandoned once they had done as much as could be expected of them. It was the challenge posed by the mammoth destruction of Nazi Germany, and the perceived threat of Soviet communist filling of that social vacuum [as indeed happened in the future Warsaw Pact countries], which inspired the Army to take the challenge of reconstruction both more seriously and more permanently. Hence the establishment of the Civil Affairs & Military Government Branch, USAR in 1955.

Subsequently Civil Affairs became increasingly involved not just in "battlefield janitor" clean-ups, but, during postwar national destabilizations, in various civic works projects (funded by American money) to try to win the discontented people's "hearts and minds". Political and social factors were studiously avoided - not just out of respect for local traditions and politics, but more frankly because CA was neither empowered nor competent to meddle in them. This is where CA has remained, doggedly but frustratingly, until the advent of MindWar.

B. Political Structures Sequence

The most stable, civilized, and pleasant societies of antiquity - such as Egypt, Crete, and Hellenic Greece - share a surprisingly simple, yet subsequently forgotten principle: that of **a *polis* defined, united, and energized by a common moral principle**.

In Egypt this was the cosmic principle or *neter* (god/ goddess) of *Maat*, usually simplified as "justice" but more precisely extending to virtue, fairness, and rectitude in all personal and community affairs. There was no concept of individual rights against the government, because government was viewed as a system ordered by the *neteru*. Similarly each Egyptian, whether high- or low-born, participated in this system. Crime and corruption were of course possible, but inadvisable because of the conviction that vice would be punished severely after Earthly death.

Virtue in Mesopotamia was understood as obedience to the willful desires of the god(s), not harmony with their natural principles. The "wrath of the gods" was feared by the state in Mesopotamia, as it was never in Egypt (which was ruled by a god-king). The Mesopotamian king sought the "right ruling" of his community, in accordance with the Akkadian principle of *Shulmu* (later adopted by the Hebrews as *Shalom*): a term meaning not just "peace" but the community well-being that engenders peace.

Hellenic Greece includes the civilizations of Crete (b. 2700 BCE), Greece (Mycenæ b. 1600 BCE, Athens b. 600 BCE), the Ægean islands, and *Magna Græcia* (Sicily and southern Italy). The Hellenic Greek cultures are most notable for exalting the intellect - for making the universe an intelligible tool and/or puzzle for mankind to explore, understand, and use. They did not conceive mankind as having a "mission" from the gods, though the gods could influence human fortunes for good or ill. To the extent that the Greeks put humanity at the "center" of importance, they worshipped its body (as in athletics and the Olympic Games) and its mind (as in the sophistic and philosophical schools of Athens).

The Cretan (Minoan) political system, a bureaucratic monarchy most significant for its peacefulness, included no evident slavery, standing military, or marked class distinctions. Women appear to have been politically equal with men. The Minoan culture was destroyed ca. 1400 BCE by an invasion from Mycenæ. The Mycenæan culture, which faded into the Greek "dark ages" within another three centuries, denied women equality and did have slavery.

The "dark ages" lasted from 1100 to 800 BCE and came to an end with the founding of the first Greek city-states. The first Greek writing appears in about the 8th century BCE, with the first dated writing in 600 BCE.

The later Hellenic era (600-300 BCE) - based as it was on empirical investigation and inductive reasoning - was a challenge to the older, tribal way of doing things. Previously custom (*nomos*) was the rule for behavior, and to follow custom was *dike*, the path of justice. Disregard of custom was *hybris* and was unacceptable and even dangerous beyond its immediate implications.

As it became increasingly evident that social problems, such as the reform of Athenian laws by Draco and then Solon, could be solved by either an appeal to either **relative practicality** or **absolute standards**, a growing controversy arose concerning the relation of *nomos* to *physis* (nature or the divine order). Foremost of the absolutists was Pythagoras, who sought in **number** the beginning or *arche* of things - the ordering principle or "one behind the many".

The teachers of relativism were known as **sophists**. There were a great many of them in Periclean Athens, and they gave advice ranging from the practical to the quasi-legal [there were no lawyers *per se*]. They performed an important function in the socialization of the community, but absolutist philosophers suspected the commercial motives behind their teaching, as well as their subordination of ideals to effectiveness. The most famous of the sophists was Protagoras (ca. 481-410 BCE), associated with the aphorism: "Man is the measure of all things." Protagoras was a materialist, holding that the explanation of all things lay in matter, but he further argued that each person perceives and interprets matter according to different perspectives. Institutions are not a manifestation of *physis*; they are conventions of human experience.

Plato (387-347 BCE) [through the character of Socrates in his *Dialogues*] considered the soul or *psyche* as the repository of the entire personality or character. One should not attempt to purify the *psyche* by rituals or restrictions, but rather to develop it through exercise of its faculties. The state is the *psyche* magnified, hence the *Republic* is most accurately seen as a prescription for the *psyche* magnified. Specifically there is a three-part similarity between state and soul: The state's populace, auxiliaries, and guardians correspond to the soul's sensation, will, and reason. The respective virtues are temperance, courage, and wisdom.

In the *Republic* Thrasymachus suggests that Justice is merely the interests of the stronger. Socrates responds that they may not know their interests. Glaucon then suggests that Justice is maximization of individual desires while avoiding suffering at others' hands. Socrates indirectly refutes this by prescribing the ideal state - the "Republic". Hence Socrates answers Thrasymachus and Glaucon by arguing that it is more natural for a man to be just rather than unjust if his soul is healthy and each part is doing its proper work.

It was important to Plato that virtue be raised to a level of **rationality**. It was not enough for people to be unconsciously or instinctively virtuous; they must "taste of the knowledge of good and evil" and then knowingly choose the good.

Plato stratified thought as *Eikasia* (primitive emotion), *Pistis* (ordinary active/reactive thinking), *Dianoia* (precise, logical, enlightened thought), and *Nœsis* (intuition and apprehension of the *Agathon*).[136]

He offered the famous "parable of the cave", whereby philosophers (who have seen the *Agathon* of perfect wisdom) lead mankind into the light by means of the *dialectic*. [Here "dialectic" means teaching or rather the

---

[136] In classical political thought there was a concern to locate authority beyond anything that anyone could appropriate, either in wisdom or in justice, or, as in the Platonic *Agathon* - the supreme Good which is beyond definition. The *Agathon* can accommodate as many formulations as there are human beings, and every person can make his own report. As there will always be a transcending or conceivable Good beyond the good(s) of particular individuals, the *Agathon* is ineffable and indefinable, and necessarily transcends the spatial and temporal limits of finite powers of perception. - Iyer, Raghavan N., *ParaPolitics: Toward the City of Man*. New York: Oxford University Press, 1979, page #22.

encouraging of self-teaching through examination and refutation of imperfect concepts.]

Plato was an elitist, but his elitism was directed towards an ideal, happy, and harmonious society, which he felt could best be attained by enlightened stratification of roles. His prescription was thus benevolent aristocracy. Critics of Plato erroneously attack him as a totalitarian oligarch. They are also bewildered by the "mysticism" which permeates his writings. Such "mysticism" is intelligible to those familiar with the Egyptian and Pythagorean metaphysics from which it derives.

The fall of the Roman Empire (an increasingly uneasy marriage of Hellenistic religious multiplicity and political pragmatism) and simultaneous ascent of institutional Christianity eclipsed the concept of the morally-defined and -sustained *polis* (of which republican Rome was arguably the last gasp), replacing it with a political order ordained by the Christian God [the "City of God/City of Man" concept articulated by Augustine (354-430 CE) and later codified into a stratification of Eternal/Natural/ Divine/Human Law by Thomas Aquinas (1225-74)]. Thus an externally-proclaimed, but intellectually-unintelligible [and unquestionable] morality governed humanity and its social institutions. This is the situation which persists today in the world's surviving theocratic cultures and states, such as those of Islam and Israel.

The cataclysm of the Protestant Reformation (1515-1648) and Catholic CounterReformation (1545-63) saw the effective elimination of theocratic political morality in Europe. It was replaced first by the Age of Absolutism (1500-1789), demarking the strongest secular monarchies, and then by the intellectual and militant revolutions of the Enlightenment (late 17th & 18th centuries). The Enlightenment proposed to replace secular monarchies with competing concepts of purely-human "social contracts" forcibly established (Thomas

Hobbes) cooperatively negotiated (John Locke), or arising from public sentiment (Jean-Jacques Rousseau). The Lockean model was that adopted by the Founding Fathers of the United States, while in the much more cynical and harsh model of Hobbes were the seeds of modern utopian socialisms, as well as Marxian communism.

Seen against this tableau, the infamous totalitarianisms of the 20th century - Italian fascism, German National Socialism, and the Marxist variations of Leninism and Maoism, were less authentic political designs than Romantic reactions against the perceived dullness and starkness of the social contract concept. Indeed by the end of that century all of the utilitarian social-contract models were exhausted, either by formal collapse (fascism, communism) or from popular disinterest and cynicism. [137]

What has gradually but inexorably replaced these ideologies is something even more impersonal and amoral: the technological society. Increasing automation and computerization of the means of production, communication, social services, finance, and military force have altered human leaders and decision-makers from ideologists to technicians. As such their effectiveness is measured not by their popularity or integrity, but rather by how well they further the technology in support of the people's continuously-rising expectations. If such a super-technician leader fails to deliver those expectations, the consequence is initially the

---

[137] We were equally tired, in mid-century, of cold sanity and hot blasphemy; of the over-cerebral and of the over-fæcal; the way out lay somewhere else. Words had lost their power either for good or for evil; still hung, like a mist, over the reality of action, distorting, misleading, castrating; but at least since Hitler and Hiroshima they were seen to be a mist, a flimsy superstructure. - Nicholas Urfe, in John Fowles' *The Magus* (op.cit.).

search for someone who promises to do so; and if this fails, explosive social instability. There is simply nothing else besides gratification to hold such a society together.[138]

Which leads this discussion to its culminative point: that what is missing from modern society, and what is thus desperately needed for it to become productive, stable, and inspiring, is **a popular morality of the very sort apparent at the beginning of ancient civilization**. This is what is meant by *ParaPolitics*, and it is what the ParaPolitics Branch of the Army exists to identify, formulate, and activate in each MW situational instance. It is the necessary end of the MW campaign, the *Agathon* towards which every decision and action within it proceeds.

C. ParaPolitics Architecture

Construction of a morally-based *polis* first requires the discarding of the ideological remnants of the "social contract" era. As Dr. Raghavan Iyer observes:

> We are especially linked to the complacent nineteenth century and its tragic aftermath. Words became infected with the ideologies of political movements on behalf of classes, elites, ruling classes, empires, and nations; and as a result we have inherited a welter of "isms" - liberalism, socialism, communism, fascism, and their prolific bastard progeny.

---

[138] This is a modern remanifestation of the "bread and circuses" atmosphere of imperial Rome, wherein the original, venerable Republican institutions had, if surviving at all, become mere sounding-boards for the emperor of the moment. The disintegration of any legislature from an active policy-making reflection of the constituent citizenry to a merely-symbolic facade for ulterior interests and motivations is an invariable harbinger of national eclipse.

No "ism" is a logically-complete and self-consistent system of ideas. Its spurious claim to completeness converts it into an ideology which can win followers and reconcile them to losses and setbacks.

An ideology is a form of imposition of holy writ by a putative expert on any doctrinal "ism", whether he or she be the guardian of a party or a church, the head of a nation or a program, or any leader who engages in an inefficient form of bossism and resorts intermittently to force, treachery, and trickery to secure compliance. This collusion initially seems adequate but in time becomes hard-hearted and precarious, and must eventually end. Demoralization results from imposition by force or fraud in lieu of inducement through a consistent appeal to the unrestricted use of reason, to common experience, and to shared insights.[139]

The problem of technology is at once simpler and more difficult to solve. Simply, it merely requires insistence that it remain subordinate to human values. The difficulty is that it is an alluring and addictive aphrodisiac for which a disillusioned, cynical populace is all too ready to sacrifice such values.[140]

The solution to this dilemma, continues Iyer, is **ParaPolitics**:

ParaPolitics signifies the imaginative application of seminal ideas vitalizing political theory and practice; the elaboration of fundamental principles into paradigms of relationships among persons and between civil means and human ends; the quest for political understanding and action

---

[139] Iyer, *op.cit.*, pages #11-12.

[140] This tension was most dramatically illustrated in Thea von Harbou's 1926 novel *Metropolis*, filmed 1927 by her husband Fritz Lang. The impasse between monstrous industrial machines and the dehumanized workers who served them was resolved only by Maria, a woman who awakened the desire for the *Agathon* in everyone - except the magician Rotwang, who sought to thwart her by creating a soulless double - the infamous robotrix *Ultima Futura* - to impersonate her. Like Kundry in Wagner's *Parsifal*, however, Maria overcame this *Doppelgänger* to redeem humanity: "The mediator between brain and hands must be the heart."

based upon expanding self-awareness; and the ever-receding perspective of ideals rooted in the ethics, metaphysics, and psychology of self-transcendence.[141]

This prescription is less formidable than it reads at first glance. Ordinary political interactions can be analytically dissected into six motivational expressions: **perfectibility**, **reason**, **welfare**, **stability**, **power**, and **self-preservation**.

The politics of perfectibility are those inspired by the desire to improve the *status quo*, whatever it may be. Reason involves established processes of discussion and negotiation, resulting in progressive changes by both consensus and compromise. Welfare considerations are those reflected within the basic fairness and humanity of various policies and proposals. Stability of the embracing social system is a constant concern with regard to all potential modifications. The quest for individual and institutional power results from personal and group ambition, and self-preservation follows from people's instinctive desire for security and continuation of their family line and community image.

In an ideal situation all six factors would be in equilibrium. In practice, particularly in the current Age of Ideologies, this is rarely if ever the case. Distortion of the principle of perfectibility leads to outbursts of patriotic narcissism along with xenophobia. Exclusive or predominant reliance upon the reasoning procedures of established institutions excuses or ignores urgent social needs which have little or no voice in them. A popular demand for welfare can leave the community stripped of its vitality by penalizing personal initiative or privilege; at extremes it leads to revolution. In contrast, an excessive concern for stability results in repressive laws and their coercive enforcement. Power for its own sake - not from

---

[141] Iyer, *op.cit.*, page #27.

the runaway idealism of perfectibility - disintegrates a community into selfishness and cynicism. Self-preservation can become overactive in a state suffering from other distortions or disruptions, resulting in personal alienation from [what remains of] the community and anarchy.

The MW diagnostic procedures of Phase 1 examine all six categories to identify both imbalances in a given area and their effect upon the entire structure. Part of the Phase 2 "cure" involves "rebalancing" that structure as efficiently and effectively as practical.

That is not where the PPB's work stops, however. It is not there just to secure a tenuous, utilitarian stability, but rather to continue into the identification and inspiration of a positive, inherently-reinforcing moral community: a true *polis*.

ParaPolitics is the twin product of **vision** and *virtu*: the former being the benevolent and creative ideas which the stabilized environment makes possible, while the latter reflects the nurturing, careful pragmatism of Machiavelli.[142] Neither "means" nor "ends" can be used to excuse the other. ParaPolitics rather demands their **identity**.

To Mahatma Gandhi this reflected the law of *karma* in politics. The end is *satya* (truth), which requires no justification. The means are *ahimsa* (non-violence). This approach presupposes that there is a transcendent morality (*Maat* or the *Agathon*) to which sincere, altruistic humans may aspire and attain.

Throughout the quest for both vision and *virtu* PPB must be guided by three interlocking, mutually-supporting energies: **will** (the strength to bring the *polis* into being), *logos* (the conviction and determination to

---

142 Cf. Chapter 10.D.

express it openly and honestly), and **eros** (deep and sincere sympathy for everyone affected by it).

Such a ParaPolitics resolution can be applied to any specific situation in any culture, geographical area, economic level, or other identifier. This is because it is applied not towards forcibly altering any of these, but simply to reduce tensions and conflicts within them and to develop their positive contributions to the *áristos*.

D. Evolution to ParaPolitics Branch

If the "brain" of a MW campaign is MWB, and the "hands" MFB, PPB is what they both exist to engender and enhance: the "heart". Once a subject group and/or area is identified as the object of a MW campaign, it is PPB which is activated to conceive, design, and nurture within it a *polis* of the highest individual and community morality: what Plato defined as *kalokagathia*.

This is no easy task, as the alienation, inadequacy, inhumanity, and resultant instability of the subject group/area are the cumulative consequence of the centuries-old suppression of this principle by the procession of exploitive, utilitarian, and alienating sociopolitical systems summarized in #B above. Furthermore PPB must tailor every such *polis* to its unique environment and circumstances, which requires sensitivity to and respect for local nonpolitical cultural traditions (for instance religion and gender customs).

The key to success in ParaPolitics is the primal yet insistent and unsuppressable impulse of humanity to **be** and **do** the Good (*Agathon*). This is the final refutation of the cold and cruel totalitarianisms which see in humanity only another natural resource to be exploited or eliminated. It further reestablishes the defining principle of a morally-progressive community: that each educated[143]   citizen is entitled to a personal formulation of relative truth, which is to be respected, not exploited or suppressed, by others.

---

[143] In this context "education" means the unfolding among receptive individuals of the capacity to choose effectively, to set themselves their standards of excellence, to exemplify tolerance and civility in relation to others, to identify with achievements and failures of those near at hand and of persons everywhere, and to see life as a process of continuous self-education. (Iyer, *op.cit.*, page #305.)

Part III: Campaign

Chapter 6: Phase ø

> The Members of the League undertake to respect and preserve as against external aggression the territorial integrity and existing political independence of all Members of the League. In the case of any such aggression or in case of any threat or danger of such aggression the Council shall advise upon the means by which this obligation shall be fulfilled.
> - Article X, Covenant of the League of Nations, 1919

> All Members shall settle their international disputes by peaceful means in such a manner that international peace and security, and justice, are not endangered. All Members shall refrain in their international relations from the threat or use of force against the territorial integrity or political independence of any state, or in any other manner inconsistent with the Purposes of the United Nations.
> - Chapter I, United Nations Charter, 1945

A. The Reality of PhysWar

Utopian appeals for an end to war, whether by international organizations, statesmen, philosophers, or artists, are abundant, eloquent, and futile. The impulse to it is too strong and pervasive throughout all human cultures and affairs: a "natural state of war" most famously observed by Thomas Hobbes (1588-1679):

> There Is Always Warre Of Every One Against Every One Hereby it is manifest, that during the time men live without a common Power to keep them all in awe, they are in that condition which is called Warre; and such a warre, as is of every man, against every man. For WARRE, consisteth not in Battell onely, or the act of fighting; but in a tract of time, wherein the Will to contend by Battell is sufficiently known:

and therefore the notion of Time, is to be considered in the nature of Warre; as it is in the nature of Weather. For as the nature of Foule weather, lyeth not in a showre or two of rain; but in an inclination thereto of many dayes together: So the nature of War, consisteth not in actuall fighting; but in the known disposition thereto, during all the time there is no assurance to the contrary. - *Leviathan*, 1651

MindWar, accordingly, does not seek to eliminate this war-impulse, but rather to divert it from a physical to a mental battlefield. The tensions, emotions, and drives remain; the physical destruction of the Earth, its resources, and its living beings does not.

While in the future MW may become the initial war-mode, at this time of its introduction and phase-in, it must expect to run into situations already destabilized and torn by PhysWar. The MWarrior, no matter how well prepared, is not entering a rational environment where both [or multiple] sides are disposed to reason. In addition to PW inertia - the continuation and escalation of PW because of economics, politics, and emotions - participants tend to the conviction that all bridges are burned: that there is no alternative to victory or annihilation. As George Orwell observed in *1984*:

War, it will be seen, accomplishes the necessary destruction, but accomplishes it in a psychologically acceptable way. In principle it would be quite simple to waste the surplus labour of the world by building temples and pyramids, by digging holes and filling them up again, or even by producing vast quantities of goods and then setting fire to them. But this would provide only the economic and not the emotional basis for a hierarchical society. What is concerned here is not the morale of masses, whose attitude is unimportant so long as they are kept steadily at work, but the morale of the Party itself. Even the humblest Party member is expected to be competent, industrious, and even intelligent within narrow limits, but it is also necessary that he should be a credulous and ignorant fanatic whose prevailing moods are fear, hatred, adulation, and orgiastic triumph. In other words it is necessary that he should have the mentality appropriate to a state of war. It does not matter whether the war is actually happening, and, since no decisive victory is possible, it does not matter whether the war is going well or badly. All that is needed is that a state of war should exist.[144]

The MWarrior entering into such an environment, therefore, has a twofold preliminary task: to identify and arrest or reduce the factors pushing for PW, and to communicate to both political leaders and PWarriors that there is a better alternative: MW.

Complicating this is that the issues in modern PWs are rarely only internal to the participant nations. More often they are resources or strategic accesses that either other nations or supranational economic institutions covet. Or it may be that the PW is the result of one or more participant nations experiencing an ideological, economic, and/or religious fragmentation.

The MWarrior's first task, therefore, is to identify and correlate all such destabilizing factors. Each element's existence and significance should be stated in terms general enough to embrace its impact on the entire situation, such that its hypothetical absence would eliminate its influence. A second reason for this generality is that it facilitates the Phase 1 diagnoses process: The "building blocks" are kept big and simple, allowing diagnosis-combinations that are easy to visualize and assemble. Examples of such factor-statements might include:

- **Participant-nation #A has too few subsistence resources to provide a minimum survival lifestyle for its people.**

---

[144] Orwell, George, "War is Peace", *1984*. New York: Harcourt, Brace & Co., 1949, page #158.

- **P-religion #B, which is universal in P-nation #C, feels threatened by different religions in P-nations #A and #D.**

- **P-ethnic group #E, diffused throughout P-nations #C and #D, feels disenfranchised in and exploited by those P-national governments, and wants its own sovereign national standing to correct this.**

- **P-nation #D feels that the only way to ensure that it won't be invaded or destroyed is to possess nuclear weapons.**

- **NonP-nations #F and #G rely upon P-nation #C for natural resource #H.**

- **NonP-nation #I needs to have the commercial route between P-nations #A and #C kept open.**

The Phase 0 list is complete when its theoretical removal would imply a peaceful, stable situation.

Completion of the Phase 0 list results in five immediate and self-evident revelations:

(1) Any one of these factors can be used to justify and trigger PW.

(2) The greater the number of factors, the higher the probability of PW.

(3) The greater the number of factors, the less the participants can even visualize, much less plan or execute a PW solution to all of them.

(4) If no alternative is available, PW will commence anyway.

(5) The onset of PW will further fragment, confuse, and complicate the original factors, so that by the time the PW concludes [if it does], the original factors will no longer be either identifiable or relevant.

These being self-evident, the usual demagogic justifications for PW evaporate, and what remains is Orwell's explanation above: that **PW is undertaken for its own sake**, not to prevent, solve, or correct anything else. MW, on the other hand, is necessarily problem-driven; it cannot function otherwise.

B. PhysWar Provocation Removal/Reversal

PW requires both an excuse for action and a calculated escalation towards that excuse. MW can expect to enter a problem situation where one or more such preliminary PW provocations are already underway. If the MW campaign is to succeed, these provocations must immediately be identified and aborted. Among the more common are:

1. Paramilitary Operations Under the Guise of "Intelligence"

"Intelligence" normally refers to the gathering and explaining of information about a problem-situation - including information which the participants don't want known. The purpose of intelligence is simply to present decision-makers with a clear, accurate, and complete picture of the situation, so that any decisions they make are not in ignorance of critical factors.

The atmosphere of secrecy in which intelligence collection efforts occur, however, has led to various agencies extending their activities into clandestine active measures such as paramilitary combat, kidnapping, and assassination. While the temptation to meddle in another nation's internal affairs is understandable, such activities violate the principle of national sovereignty and destroy the intruder's image as an open and honest international participant. "Intelligence" must be limited to intelligence.

2. Emotion-Arousing Violence

While the term "terrorism" has been overused to mean merely any individual or group resisting any participant-nation's government control, its original meaning was the employment of "terror" (e.g. intimidating or violent actions designed to frighten both recipients and witnesses into silence and cooperation). [The term "state terrorism" identifies similar behavior by established governments.]

A campaign of terror is meant to convince the recipients that the government cannot or will not protect them, while on the other hand failure to cooperate with the terrorists will result in punishment or death.

As the government and/or any occupying forces cannot know where such terrorists will strike next, they cannot be defeated in the conventional sense. Rather they must be neutralized by removing their motivation, be it religious, ideological, ethnic, etc. This is a task for strategic MWB applications.

A key element of terror is its indiscrimination. It injures or kills persons not just directly, but also randomly and incidentally. Hence the terrorist's weapons of choice are imprecise and remote ones: roadside explosives, suicide vests, boobytraps, and [in state terrorism] missiles, aircraft bombs, and drones. The terrorizing of the affected populace is in no small part because it is aware that even the most docile conduct is no guarantee of safety. Terror becomes the way of daily life, with commensurate physical and psychological toll.

3. False-Flag Operations

Governments kill, or allow to be killed, their own people when it is deemed necessary to create popular fear of and antagonism towards a scapegoat target which has itself not committed any such act. History is replete with examples, exposed or still clouded in deception and suspicion.

While obvious effective in producing the immediately-desired effect, false-flags are, ethically, despicable and shameful. Such actions must be absolutely rejected as a policy option, and when discovered exposed and punished without excuse, evasion, or equivocation.

4. Drum-Beating

A lie repeated frequently and forcefully enough will eventually be popularly accepted as "truth" unless it is quickly exposed and refuted. While again an effective PW-agitating device, this procedure violates the simple standard of truth and honesty. Countering "the big lie" is again a MWB strategic task.

5. Population Repression

Governmental limitation or removal of civil liberties and rights on the grounds that this is necessary to "fight terrorism" does nothing to deter terrorists (who will not respect any such limitations), but it will both aggravate the populace towards the scapegoat and discourage protest against the PW-promotion. The more a populace is prevented from articulating dissent and alternative courses of action, the more it can be goaded into PW-fervor.

6. Degradation of the Individual

In Chapter 1 the First and Second Laws of MW recognize and respect the dignity of each human being, regardless of his place within the overall MW campaign. His bodily mechanisms and thought-processes are accessed only non-injuriously, for the sole purpose of inclining and inducing him to cooperate with and contribute to attainment of the *áristos* and subsequent ParaPolitical *polis*.

In a PW environment, on the other hand, the individual is dehumanized into "the enemy", whereupon "it" can be shot, beaten, kidnapped, tortured, exiled, imprisoned, and/or killed. If any of this happens by accident, it is mere "collateral damage" of no more consequence than [if anything] a token cash payment to surviving family. The history of PW is the dark legacy of man the Killer Angel's contempt for life.

Indeed what is ultimately at issue here is the very phenomenon of life itself. Either it is a "divine spark" to be revered and protected, or it is nothing more than an accidental meat-machine to be exploited or exterminated as desired. There is no middle-ground between these alternatives.

C. MindWar Integrity

A MW campaign cannot succeed if "the house be divided against itself". PW pressures, both overt and covert, over which the United States and other participants have control, must be arrested before a MW solution can be initiated. Otherwise the MW campaign will be assumed to be a sham: a mere show-distraction from the actual PW agenda. Indeed it is the suspension of all PW-pressures, albeit temporarily and provisionally, which gives the MW campaign its initial dignity and credibility.

PW-habitués may deride the rigorously-idealistic taboos above as naïve, wishful thinking in today's harsh world of routine callousness and cruelty. "Nice guys", they will insist, "finish last." Nevertheless if humanity is to be brought back from the brink of self-annihilation, it can only be by a conviction of honesty, empathy, and humanitarianism so resolute that all such cynicism shatters before it. Nowhere is this better argued than by Albert Camus in a letter to a German friend while serving in the French Resistance during World War II:

> You never believed in the meaning of this world, and you therefore deduced the idea that everything was equivalent and that good and evil could be defined according to one's wishes. You supposed that in the absence of any human or divine code the only values were those of the animal world - in other words, violence and cunning. Hence you concluded that man was negligible and that his soul could be killed, that in the maddest of histories the only pursuit for the individual was the adventure of power and his only morality, the realism of conquests. And, to tell the truth, I, believing I thought as you did, saw no valid argument to answer you

except a fierce love of justice which, after all, seemed to me as unreasonable as the most sudden passion.

Where lay the difference? Simply that you readily accepted despair and I never yielded to it. Simply that you saw the injustice of our condition to the point of being willing to add to it, whereas it seemed to me that man must exalt justice in order to fight against eternal injustice, create happiness in order to protest against the universe of unhappiness. Because you turned your despair into intoxication, because you freed yourself from it by making a principle of it, you were willing to destroy man's works and to fight him in order to add to his basic misery. Meanwhile, refusing to accept that despair and that tortured world, I merely wanted men to rediscover their solidarity in order to wage war against their revolting fate.

As you can see, from the same principles we derived quite different codes. Because you were tired of fighting heaven, you chose injustice and sided with the gods. I, on the contrary, chose justice in order to remain faithful to the world. I continue to believe that this world has no ultimate meaning. But I know that something in it has a meaning, and that is man, because he is the only creature to insist on having one. This world has at least the truth of man, and our task is to provide its justifications against fate itself. And it has no justification but man; hence he must be saved if we want to save the idea we have of life. With your scornful smile you will ask me: What do you mean by saving man? And with all my being I shout to you that I mean not mutilating him and yet giving a chance to the justice that man alone can conceive.[145]

Hence such "clearing of the field" is not as fanciful as it might seem. It is clearly in the interests of all participants to avoid the death and destruction of PW, and MW is the most methodical and practical means for realizing this.

---

[145] Albert Camus, 4th Letter to a German Friend, July 1944. Camus (1913-1960) was a French philosopher who received the 1957 Nobel Prize for Literature "for his important literary production, which with clear-sighted earnestness, illuminates the problems of the human conscience in our times".

If one or more participants refuse to halt their PW efforts, the MW Command (MWC) assembled to assess and activate the MW campaign may decline to proceed further. The situation then reverts to previous PW-oriented authorities and agendæ.

This acceptance or rejection of MW capability also highlights the limitations of a MW apparatus constructed solely within the U.S. Army. Ideally MW should emanate as policy from the highest levels of government, with the Army's MWC finding the diplomatic and pre-PW field already cleared for it when a situation is designated. Instead this experimental Army component must anticipate "Phase 0", in which it must discover and attempt to bring to a halt ongoing PW pressures. Within the MW structure this is principally a task for the MFB, since it possesses both the mobility to examine the subject area and the versatility to avoid dangerous confrontations while doing so.

Phase 0 concludes when MFB reports its findings to the MWC, which then makes the decision either to proceed to Phase 1 or to reject the MW assignment.

Given the abundance and strength of pre-PW forces resisting MW, is MW worth pursuing? The answer to this must be sought in the innate character of mankind. If de Sade correctly asserted the human race to be motivated by and committed to its self-destruction, then, as Hobbes predicted, we are condemned to a future which is "nasty, brutish, and short".

But if, as Abraham Lincoln believed, there are "better angels of our nature" whom we may summon to inspire our compassion for and behavior towards one another, then MW is not naïve idealism but an eminently worthwhile and achievable virtue. Where it can be brought to bear, it must be.

Chapter 7: Phase 1

> To win one hundred victories in one hundred battles is not
> the acme of skill. To subdue the enemy without fighting is
> the acme of skill.
>
> > \- Sun Tzu

> Defeat is a state of mind. No one is ever defeated until defeat
> has been accepted as a reality. To me, defeat in anything is
> merely temporary, and its punishment is but an urge for me
> to greater effort to achieve my goal. Defeat simply tells me
> that something is wrong in my doing; it is a path leading to
> success and truth.
>
> > \- Bruce Lee

A. Redefinition of the Problem

MW Phase 1 is the redefinition of an assigned conflict
in terms of an acceptable and practical outcome.

The U.S. armed forces are not accustomed to foreign
involvements leading to anything less than complete
destruction of the assigned enemy. A MW campaign
begins with the elasticity of outcome: a solution which is
the best possible under the circumstances (*áristos*),
though it may not completely satisfy any participant in
the conflict. The *áristos* may well justify medals, but
probably not triumphal parades.

The nascent PW halted in Phase ø is characterized not
only by its covert mischief but also by its official
misrepresentation, if not outright denial. Attacks and
invasions take place under monikers of "peacekeeping",
"stabilization", or "assistance", either U.S.-unilaterally or

under the umbrella of the United Nations, NATO, or "coalitions". This evasive labeling fools no one, but adds to the general confusion in that neither actors nor goals are openly and clearly acknowledged. And since they aren't, no one knows what the PW goal is, how to determine whether it's reached, or even who would make such a determination.

B. Declaration of MindWar

MW begins with a formal declaration of MindWar, which includes a definition of the problem and identification of its participants, as well as a proposal for [collective] victory (*áristos*). Ideally this should happen in the Congress, per a formal declaration under the Constitution's Article I §8, although in a post-World War II era of unending PW actions both overt and covert, Congress has largely abandoned this responsibility to the Presidency. The introduction of MW gives Congress an excellent opportunity to reassert its authority, since MW is a humanitarian solution unlikely to generate the domestic political emotions and pressures caused by PW actions. Quite the contrary, the citizenry is likely to stand predominantly, if not unanimously behind such an forthright approach to an international problem.

Another benefit of a formal MW declaration is that it signals to the situation-country or its internal conflicting groups that the United States as an entity is committed to a MW solution; it is not a "house divided" in which an ostensible MW campaign may be undermined by a continuing covert PW one. It also informs such participants what general solution the United States has in mind, so that they can begin to discuss its effectiveness and acceptability among themselves. The PW alternative, obviously, promises only indeterminate death and destruction.

Assuming, however, that it will take some time [and some evidence of less-formal MW successes] before Congress is emboldened to this formal extent, U.S. Army MW itself must define its MW mission and sell it progressively to the Army, the Defense Department, and other concerned governmental departments and agencies. This is rather less daunting than it sounds, since such external governmental entities are generally willing to "give MW enough rope" as long as they are not responsible for a failed campaign. MW, as previously discussed, is completely prepared for the possibility of failure, although, like Bruce Lee, it regards obstacles as incentives to rechart the path to the *áristos*. "You **can** get there from here."

C. Diagnosis of the "Disease"

The symptom of PW is military or guerrilla action by or within a situation-location. There can be many reasons for such eruption of violence, and often several simultaneously: livelihood hardship, fear of harm [whether from the government, invading/occupying forces, or guerrillas], anger from experienced harm, religious fanaticism, individual or sectarian political ambition, territorial greed, and/or involuntary impressment.

What might initially startle conventional intelligence officers and strategic planners is that the MW diagnostic procedures below are conducted unclassified and completely in the open. It is essential to the accuracy of all the steps, as well as to the final Foundation Diagnosis (FD), that as many of the individuals, groups, and organizations included in the diagnostic sweep be aware of it and have the opportunity to both critique and contribute to it. This reflects the MW principle that a successful MW campaign must be waged by all participants against inertial PW pressures, and that the only true MW victory is a collective one.

1. Internal Diagnosis

Before evaluating a U.S. MW response to a specific situation, the MW strategist must identify all contributing irritants - in the absence of any U.S. interference whatever - and create a profile of the situation-location accordingly. It would be convenient if such irritants could be given neat, numerical weights and plotted on a mathematical matrix, but this is impossible due to their fundamental dissimilarities. What **is** possible is to rank them in rough order of their influence; for instance in one country religion may be the dominant aggravation, while in another only a minor consideration.

Internal national policies, customs, or issues, such as race, nonnational ethnic groups, gender status, civil rights, which may indirectly bear upon PW brinksmanship, must also be identified and ranked.[146]

Such a gradient is completed for each participant group. Then the groups with their rankings are placed side-by-side in a lineup to compare motivations and their relative influence. Similarities in strong influences suggest what a MW campaign must emphasize in order to succeed - if the situation-location exists in complete isolation, which in most situations it does not.

---

[146] PW has always been sold to people in grandiose absolutes: the freeing of an oppressed country, vengeance for a claimed outrage, the establishment of democracy, etc. MW, on the other hand, limits its objectives, and its claims, to the possible and the practical, which may be significantly short of the ideal, as well as more difficult to explain. In short, at its best MW is not emotionally satisfying.

2. External Diagnosis

The next step of diagnosis is to similarly identify and rank all external influences bearing upon the impending or aborted PW in which the situation-location is engaged either internally or externally. This must be done for each foreign country whose policies or actions contribute to the PW momentum, as well as for involved non-national organizations or enterprises. Again a ranked lineup is created, and a weighted picture generated. At this level of analysis, care must also be taken to identify whether specific foreign countries' interests are aligned or antagonistic to one another. In short, the situation-location may actually be an artificial proxy for a much larger, indirect contest.

During the Cold War many "wars of national liberation" were regarded by the capitalist and communist blocs as showcase tests of their worldwide power and prestige. Such views were not necessarily shared by the local client regimes or movements. Vietnam's Ho Chi Minh, for example, was first and foremost an anticolonialist who admired and cited the American Declaration of Independence. Only when he perceived American support for the post-World War II restoration of French colonialism did he turn to the Soviet Union and China, allies with whom his regime maintained an uneasy and mistrustful relationship, exploding eventually into Vietnam's 1979 war with China.

An obvious danger here is unconscious analytical bias in favor of the United States and/or its favored international clients; or against countries, blocs, or non-national groups or influences perceived or imagined to be hostile to the U.S. Diagnosis must be objective and dispassionate if it is to be accurate. During later MW Phases applicable biases and agendæ can and should be acknowledged and faced, but never in Phase 1.

3. Composite Diagnosis

Once both internal and external lineups have been completed, they are combined into a composite, whereupon overall common factors are identified and ranked. While this stage of analysis may begin with a simple diagram, it cannot end there, because this is the stage at which MW situation-location population analysis comes into play. Strategic research & analysis teams from all three MW branches must consult towards an *áristos* path which not only participant leaders but the affected populace may agreeably and realistically tread.

4. Analysis Expertise

Formal area- and country-studies abound within the various departments and agencies of the U.S. government, as do published books, periodicals, and running commentaries in the commercial media and Internet. For a MW diagnosis the R&A teams must cast their net as widely as possible, again taking care not to exclude or discount facts or points of view which the United States might find politically, economically, or emotionally inconvenient or repugnant.[147]

5. Foundation Diagnosis

Finally the MW R&A teams produce a comprehensive diagnosis, which, once articulated, will be the foundation of the consequent MW campaign. This Foundation Diagnosis (FD) is the source to which all operational

---

[147] The Schrödinger's Cat problem: There is inherent difficulty in a national analysis being performed objectively from within the nation itself, because its traditions, norms, beliefs and taboos tend to be taken for granted and hence unrealized as relevant, significant factors - and thus not to be considered changeable ones.

elements of the campaign - MWB, MFB, and PPB - will constantly refer to ensure the coordination and success of the campaign. It is a dynamic, continuously-updated resource, not a static document.[148]

D. Prescription of the "Cure": The *Áristos*

The FD, if correctly done, presents the present profile of the situation-location and provides indices which can be used for short, medium, or long-range forecasts as well. Any one of a number of social, political, and economic forecasting techniques can be applied to the FD, but these will only indicate the situation-location's future if the present destabilizing influences which have caused the PW environment are left unchanged.[149] It is the purpose of a MW campaign to change them in such a way as to eliminate the threat of PW and ensure a stable, constructive, and endurable environment. The word "peace" is intentionally not used, because it may be necessary to continue the formal state of MW significantly past the initial elimination of violence into correction of the imbalances which could otherwise lead

---

[148] The name of this culminate, operational diagnosis pays tribute to Isaac Asimov's *Foundation* series of science-fiction novels, in which two Foundations were established to minimize galactic social decay and disintegration through psychohistorical analysis and counteractive measures.

[149] A comprehensive and readable survey of political, social, & economic forecasting theory and techniques is *Futuring: The Exploration of the Future* by Edward Cornish (Bethesda: World Future Society, 2004). Cornish, who Edits *The Futurist* magazine for the WFS, has constantly revised and updated this primer at least since I first discovered it in 1977 [as *The Study of the Future*]. MWarriors, after initial orientation at the JFK Center and graduate studies in magic at the Magic Castle and in *kung fu* at the Shaolin Monastery, may further expand their professional acumen through WFS curricula.

to its return. Formal MW victory is declared when the situation-location can be left to function completely without it.

1. The MW Campaign Goal: the *Áristos*

From the FD MWB strategists develop a goal for the MW campaign. This goal represents the most practical, quick, and universally-endurable changes which can be made to the FD in order to alter its profile to one of non-PW stability. Thus this goal is called the *áristos*, the ancient Greek term signifying "the best for a given situation".[150]

The *áristos* is not ready-made; it does not present itself from the FD, because the FD is merely a profile of the unaltered situation and a means to forecast from it. The *áristos* is an intrusion into the FD inertia, an adjustment of it to alter it. If the FD is done correctly, it will not be easy to alter it in a manner which does not risk unexpected ripple-effects, some of which could engender new instabilities. For this reason the correct *áristos* will be one which stabilizes the problem-situation with minimum disruption of the FD.

2. Flexibility of the Weighted Ranked Factors

The diagnostic process produced ranked diagnostic factors which combined with analytical expertise led to the fusion of the FD. The next step towards the development of the *áristos* is to evaluate each factor in terms of how quickly and easily [if at all] it may be changed. Once the quickest & easiest possible adjustments are identified, the question becomes which

---

[150] The concept of the *áristos* may be studied in numerous contexts and applications in John Fowles' *The Áristos* (Boston: Little, Brown & Company, 1964).

combination of these would suffice to stabilize the problem-situation most easily, practically, and economically.

3. Open Access Evaluation

In PW opposing sides plan their strategies in secret, seeking to surprise, deceive, and disadvantage one another. Since each side is necessarily working with an incomplete and distorted picture of the situation, intelligence (the attempted acquisition of information an opponent wishes to conceal) is essential, inevitably with incomplete and imperfect results. The consequence is a PW campaign of misunderstandings, mistakes, blunders, and excesses: the sum-total of which does not, indeed cannot lead to a rational resolution of the conflict.

In MW the process leading to the FD is not only not classified, but is advertised and open to all conflict participants. **The "enemy" is the PW-conducive situation, not any individual or group caught up in it.** While the FD is initiated, developed, assembled, formatted, and disseminated by assigned U.S. Army MW strategic R&A teams, access to and suggestions regarding their deliberations are actively, constantly sought and welcomed. Situation participants not only have the most direct and convenient access through electronic media, but are invited to visit the strategic MWC headquarters to meet and dialogue with the MW planners themselves.

The result is a FD as complete and undistorted as possible, and an emerging *áristos* which is neither a surprise nor an emotional confrontation to anyone involved. If a less-than-ideal solution were sprung as a surprise by only one side in a conflict, the odds for its acceptance would be reduced by the opponent's pride and resentment of a "dictated ultimatum". If, as in MW, everyone takes both the credit and the blame for a tolerable if imperfect *áristos*, such emotional coloring is minimized, possibly completely avoided.

4. Acceptance of the *Áristos*

Before the MW campaign can be activated on the basis of the FD and its emergent *áristos*, all situation participants must agree that it is acceptable. This is of course much easier if they have all been involved in the process from which it emerges, in that they were thus able to propose and evaluate alternative solutions.

Planning participants, however, are not the only ones who must agree to the *áristos*. Each must present it to superiors, subordinates, and general adherents, and secure their endorsement and cooperation. This will usually be tentative and reluctant, because that is the nature of an *áristos*. As the MW campaign proceeds, acceptance of the *áristos* should solidify. If it begins to dissolve, it is a sign that the *áristos* was wrongly formulated and needs redefinition.

Chapter 8: Phase 2

In the province of connected minds, what the network believes to be true is true or becomes true within certain limits to be found experientially and experimentally. These limits are further beliefs to be transcended. In the network's mind there are no limits.

- John C. Lilly

The war was an unnecessary condition of affairs, and might have been avoided if forbearance and wisdom had been practiced on both sides.

- Robert E. Lee

Once the Foundation Diagnosis (FD) has been initially formulated [as it is a dynamic, not a static document] and the *áristos* determined, Phase 2 reverse-engineers that *áristos* from its achievement to the present situation. The purpose of this is to identify what changes, in what sequence and/or combination, are necessary to attain the *áristos*.

As each such change is identified, the assets, forces, and resources necessary to effect it are specified. If for any deficiency the change is deemed unachievable, the reverse-engineering seeks an alternative path around it to the FD. If no such path can be found, the *áristos* is unattainable as presently defined and must be revised less ambitiously until a practical path to the FD is achievable.

The problem-situation cannot, of course, be relied upon to remain static while the MW campaign's incremental changes are being applied. As each change occurs, the FD must be updated accordingly, along with the reverse-engineered [and now presumably shorter] path to the *áristos*.

Another consideration in all social engineering is the "law of unintended consequences", by which any change, or even the existing situation *per se*, may mutate suddenly and unexpectedly due to unforeseen events, such as assassinations of key individuals, crises in nearby environments, or natural disasters. Such surprises do not automatically dismantle the MW campaign, but they must be absorbed into it and compensated for if/when they occur.

The result of Phase 2 reverse-engineering is a "map to the *áristos*" which all MW operational elements must follow if proper coordination is to be attained and the *áristos* realized. If the "map" is constructed correctly, its success will be inevitable, because it is based not only on physical situations and conditions, but on **the mechanism of the minds of all humans involved**. It is this latter feature of the MW campaign which distinguishes it from a conventional "reallocation of resources" analysis, such as is both commonplace and useless in international disputes. In MW the psychology of all participants is the missing key which not only makes the campaign possible but makes its outcome inevitable.

A. Task Organization and Composition

Phase 2 requires a major reconceptualization of the old U.S. Army MISO unit design and functionality.

In the old MISO configuration, which was designed for PW battlefield-janitor support, the only strategic units were two Active Army MISO groups (MISOGs) located at Fort Bragg, NC under a single MISO command (MISOC). The USAR units scattered around the United States consisted of tactical elements only, suitable for deployment in support of committed PW operations.[151]

Within the MISOC, responsibility for strategic MISO research & analysis rested with a Cultural Intelligence Element (CIE) which, since it was limited to a few 2-year-contracted civilians who are all deployable overseas, could not possibly attract either the extensive experience, all-source information collection, or academic discipline expertise essential to MW.[152]

Under MW configuration, strategic research & analysis responsibility is a USAR function. Strategic MWB groups (MWBGs) are assigned general geographic areas of responsibility. To monitor these in time of peace, and perform MW diagnoses in times of developing conflict, these MWBGs create a varying number of specialized MWB diagnostic teams (MWBTs), located near government departments/ agencies, universities, and private-sector research institutions specializing on the geographic areas in question. These MWBTs are fixed/non-deployable, and are composed of both highly-specialized and -credentialed USAR soldiers and contract civilians. When a MW campaign is formally declared, the

---

[151] The two USAR MISO Groups (the 2nd & 7th) were proposed to be brought into the MISOC in Fiscal Year 2013, with their missions revised as well.

[152] "The Cultural Intelligence Element (CIE), formerly known as the Strategic Studies Detachment, is an organic part of the MISOC that provides in-depth analyses of cultural, social, political, and historical factors affecting MISO as well as lethal and nonlethal operations. The CIE offer doctor of philosophy (Ph.D.)-level subject-matter expertise and advice on mission planning, impacts, and ramifications to supported commanders, U.S. COMs, and deployed MISO forces. The CIE consists of deployable civilian members educated and experienced in Political Science, History, Cultural Anthropology, and other social and behavioral sciences, with a high-level of foreign language capability. The CIE also provides long-term institutional and operational support to MISBs and U.S. country teams." - Department of the Army FM 3-53, *MISO*, January 2013, ¶3-34.

MWBG with that geographic focus is responsible for producing its Foundation Diagnosis (FD) and updating it throughout the campaign until victory is declared in Phase 4.

This MWBG has tasking authority directly to the MetaForce teams (MFTs) already in the situation-location, requiring them to both provide on-site feedback for the FD and also to identify and secure the participation of key actors within the conflict. In order to do this efficiently, tactical MWBTs (which are the function of the Active Army MWBGs) are deployed with the MFTs. Their specific mission is to raise the MW diagnosis to its most accurate level, and to both guide and facilitate the MFTs in their actions enhancing the MW campaign. **The mission of the MWB and its MWBTs is to establish a mental environment making the success of the MFTs inexorable and inevitable. Nothing is left to chance. Before any MFT proceeds with MW Phase 3, its path must be cleared of all mental obstacles to its success.**

Once the MW Command (MWC) approves the FD, it task-organizes its assets to implement it.

MW units are all team-modular, so appropriate teams can be instantly reassigned to create a task-focused unit. The level of the created unit depends upon the complexity of its component of the FD.

B. Time and Space Parameters

Before the *áristos* can be reverse-engineered, its implementation must be defined in terms of both time and space. These terms have a substantially different meaning and significance in MW than they do in PW:

1. Time

In the old PW universe, "time" was merely a clocking of the expenditure of assets towards the subjugation of humans labeled as enemies, and the annihilation or occupation of their lands and livelihoods. This clock began with D-Day and ended with V-Day; or rather it was then eventually reset to the next decided D-Day.

For the MWarrior, however, "time" is not a clocking device, but rather a problem-identifying and -defining one. It is "time", indeed, which more than any other single factor, generates, sustains, and concludes modern human conflicts. The reason for this is that today's human beings are motivated to action not by an "endless present" but by their vision, expectation, and promise of the future.

This is a relatively recent development. The ancient Egyptians, for instance, sought perfection in stability, harmony, symmetry, geometry, and a cyclical [as opposed to a progressive or linear] concept of time. A similar interpretation of time characterized the Maya, the Greeks, and China.

Later the Hebrews and Christians introduced a linear concept, containing both a beginning and an end to time. The consequence of this was to demand of mankind a "mission": a mandatory, desperate march towards that end.[153]

Originally such a linear enslavement of humanity was thought to be dictated by God, with posthumous reward or punishment awaiting each Jew, Christian, or Muslim in accordance with his obedience and accomplishment. With the onset of the Enlightenment in the 17th/18th centuries C.E., literal belief in God and eschatology faded

---

[153] Cf. G.J. Whitrow, *The Nature of Time*. New York: Oxford University Press, 1972.

into metaphor, but the concept of linear progress persisted. Now, however, the impetus was towards a human-created utopian society in this life; and various "social contract" ideologies to attain it - such as socialism, capitalism, fascism, and communism - competed for popular emotional endorsement and commitment.

What has changed with the end of the 20th century is what might be called "the death of Hope". Neither God nor man is believed any longer as a creator of Paradise, either here or hereafter, so what has superseded both is a worldwide culture of temporal gratification: wealth, power, prestige, and glamor. The only "immortality" is to successfully make one's mark in history: to manage to write "Kilroy Was Here" on the Great Mandala of history as it sweeps through and past one's brief lifetime.[154]

The significance of this to MW is that while the United States and similar "postmodern" cultures mock time in this hedonistic *danse macabre*, many enclaves of the world experiencing social disruption still exist in the old utopian, or even-older metaphysical time-contexts. If the MWarrior does not recognize and address this, he will completely misunderstand the perceptions and motivations of the subject-locale inhabitants.

During the Cold War, Western strategists thought to defeat communists with promises of capitalist affluence, failing to understand that Marxism sees such [class-characteristic] luxuries as merely superficial diversions from a universal utopia.

In the 21st century the same stimulus-strategists find themselves mystified by the intensity of Muslim fanaticism, failing once again to understand that this is their sincere vision of the perfect future - just as modern Israel, no less than its ancient model, sees its political

---

[154] With inexorable appreciation to Peter, Paul, and Mary for "The Great Mandala (The Wheel of Life)" (Peter Yarrow, Pepamar Music Corp., 1967).

future not as negotiated by men, but as commanded by YHVH.

When visualizing a MW campaign, therefore, it must be in both the time-context and the time-expectations of the subject populace and its leadership. This may range from a Western-imitative contempt for time, to fierce fundamentalist eschatology: a passionate conviction that the End of All is imminent.

Once the governing time-parameter has been ascertained, it can be manipulated to serve the *áristos* by seizing control of its own defining mechanisms. If an ideology, reinterpret its implementation - as Lenin did when he revised Marxism into his "dictatorship of the proletariat". If a resurgent religious fundamentalism, advance a vision of even greater intensity, purity, and redemption to coopt it - as first Christianity and later Islam did with Judaism, and as Protestantism would also do with medieval Catholicism.

The blind fury of such passion is by no means limited to modern Islam, as for instance the previously cited Thirty Years' War engulfing almost the entire European subcontinent in an overwhelming bloodbath.

The common feature of all the linear-time doctrines, whether supernatural or secular, is their promise of Paradise. They offer the Hope which disillusioned, sybaritic modernity has abandoned. The MWarrior should not - indeed cannot - kill this Hope. Quite the contrary: Like Pandora in the ancient Greek legend, he should safeguard and nurture it as one of the strongest of MW assets.[155]

2. Space

What dimensions does the *áristos* embrace in terms of national geography, dispersion of ethnic groups, livelihood resources? Here a balance must be struck: If the expanses are too large, MW resources will not be able to support them. If they are too small, attainment of the *áristos* will be overwhelmed by uncontrolled exterior influences and forces.

What is presently referred to as the "nation-state system" came into being gradually and incrementally in European history, but is generally assumed to have stabilized into its modern semblance with the Treaty of Westphalia (1648). While "nation" identifies an ethnic or cultural group, "state" identifies a sovereign geographic area. The combined entity has since been assumed to have international legitimacy and recognition as a "unit" of global humanity.

Complicating this, of course, have been many inconvenient historical developments, such as rising ethnic identities across state borders, religious movements, nonstate ideologies (such as socialism and communism), and most recently transnational capitalist economic enterprise. While the nation-state system still clings to many traditions of sovereignty, such as war, taxation, and internal law, it is clearly a concept in

---

[155] Pandora was the first human woman, created by the gods of Mount Olympus and entrusted with a jar which she was warned never to open. Eventually her curiosity overcame her and she violated the prohibition, releasing all of the evils of the world to afflict humanity forevermore. But also in the jar the gods had placed Hope, who made it possible to endure and survive those evils. The Greeks would have considered the modern "death of Hope" as a dark omen indeed.

inexorable, if not yet terminal disintegration. Its evolutionary successor will most likely be some form of corporate plutocracy, with the old countries lingering merely as human-control mechanisms for internal policing and external warmaking.

The United States, as the world's sole surviving superstate, has by default become the defender and enforcer of the nation-state concept, while simultaneously, by virtue of the multinational economic entities it has engendered, it is ironically also its psychopomp. Appropriately the United States' official enemies in the 21st century are no longer other nation-states, but nonstate individuals and groups who disregard or threaten that idol of legitimacy and sovereignty. Such individuals and groups are currently called "terrorists".[156]

The dilemma of the 21st-century environment, obviously, is that the United States' announced policy of "non-negotiation with terrorists" constricts it to only one course of action: their PW extermination. In a world in which non-nation-state groups are rapidly and massively proliferating, while the 17th-century state structures are fighting a commensurately-desperate and Quixotic battle to cling to their old *Weltanschauung*, this is a naïve and ultimately futile intransigence.

The MWarrior must not only be willing to negotiate with **anyone**; he must actively initiate and facilitate such dialogue. As the identities and positions of those with whom he interacts may not [and probably won't] be nation-state credentialed, the operative concept of the physical entity at issue will change as well to accurately encompass the problem. It is this problem which MWB

---

[156] If an established, internationally-recognized nation-state develops an uncooperative or inconvenient government, it may be propagandistically denied legitimacy as a "rogue state", whereupon it is acceptable to force "regime change" upon it.

and MFB must reidentify as the common enemy to be conquered by all human participants.

C. Reverse-Engineering the *Áristos*

Once the time and space parameters for the *áristos* have been defined, the material and psychological requirements for its attainment are addressed:

1. Material Requirements

When conflict arises over the ownership, control, and use of resources, there are two general solutions: reallocation of the existing supply and/or addition to that supply, eliminating or lessening the need for reallocation. The former is more possible within a sovereign nation-state; the primary problem is the willingness of owning/controlling interests to reduce their share and the amount of such reduction necessary to satisfy the demands of the populace.

Complicating this question is the modern fluidity of both variables: Both resources and people are constantly moving in and out of the situation environment. What is needed, therefore, is not an arrangement of fixed quantities, but rather a formula which will move along with both variables.

Such formulas since the Enlightenment have generally aligned into the ideologies of capitalism (private ownership) and socialism (government ownership), with communism (collective ownership) and anarchism (no ownership) being extreme if unsustainable alternatives.

Capitalism's attraction is that it stimulates efficiency through competition and opportunism. Socialism removes the motive of personal greed and gratification, replacing it with overall common security. Human beings nevertheless continue to desire and seek advantage over one another, and in socialistic systems this takes the form of bureaucratic competition and aggrandizement. "Capitalism is the exploitation of man by man," it is said, "while socialism is the reverse."

Social-contract ideology, accordingly, is not an answer to resources tension. What is needed is an atmosphere of altruism within whatever the ideological framework happens to be. This is not an economic or a resource commitment, but an emotional one: the *kalokagathia* of the morally-based *polis*. It is the task of MWB to incline the mental dispositions of all participants towards this emotion through appropriate combinations of the PSYCONs detailed in Chapter 3, the concurrent task of MFB to encourage all involved individuals and groups to manifest this good will in concrete, constructive expression of the *áristos*, and the task of PPB to develop and communicate a vision of community perfection beyond the immediate *áristos* which will enthuse, energize, and sustain the new moral *polis*.

The inculcation of leader and popular enthusiasm towards a visionary goal is nothing new in history; it characterizes everything from football games to national revolutions. The common feature of such ordinary expressions, however, is their vagueness and lack of substance. Once the initial burst of passionate ecstasy dissipates, the old alienations and selfish divisions reassert themselves. Only the labels [if even that] are different.

The reverse-engineering from the *áristos* stability to the present instability is governed by the simple principle of need. What is most essential to all affected individuals' survival and safety is what is prioritized, from initial emergency relief at present to a gradually more affordable and sustainable minimum. Care must be taken not to overrun this minimum, otherwise expectations will promptly rise to the excess; and if that excess is not sustainable, fresh tensions will result.

Once critical material needs have been identified and prioritized, supplementary ones are added as availability and practicality permit. Along with subsistence, people desire comfort, pleasure, and dignity. Much of this can be improved modestly and incrementally. As long as attention and improvement are seen and experienced, the populace will not be in as much of a hurry for it as for survival and safety essentials.

2. Psychological Requirements

In a successful MW campaign it is not just what changes are reverse-engineered to take place, but how they are explained, how affected individuals and groups feel welcome and empowered to respond to and influence them, and ultimately what contribution they make to the complete cooperative and moral climate of the emerging *polis*.

Psychological reverse-engineering also follows the principle of need. In a present-moment condition of physical privation and danger, ideological and egotistical concerns are extraneous; what matters is to save lives, alleviate fear, and eliminate hunger and disease. The mechanisms for accomplishing these are not reserved to either capitalism or socialism, though their exercise under each may differ in organization and image.

Only when all vital needs have been met and stabilized is it time for the character of the future *polis* to be addressed. In the previous PW environment this was a tediously-familiar cabaret: the *cliché* harangues of capitalist/socialist platitudes. In MW it is irrelevant which model nominally triumphs; the essential determinant is which one best facilitates the development of the *polis*. As one experienced adjuster of international tensions observed:

> Of course patriotism comes along and makes it seem fairly all right, but this "my country right or wrong" business is getting a little out of date. Today we are fighting communism. Okay. If I'd been alive fifty years ago, the brand of conservatism we have today would have been damn near called communism, and we should have been told to go and fight that. History is moving pretty quickly these days, and heroes and villains keep changing parts. [157]

It is the mandate of ParaPolitics to take human moral community-building to the next social-evolutionary stage beyond the timeworn social-contract ideologies of the last two centuries. As in the science-fictional *Metropolis*, the key to this will be found not in utilitarian mechanisms of production and wealth, nor in deceptive schemes of demagogic conformity, but by recognition of and respect for the innate desire of mankind to be and do the Good: the Platonic *Agathon*. Metaphysically this is the true Quest for the Grail, which ParaPolitics renders both visible and attainable.

Phase 2 of the MW campaign is never "finally" complete, since it is subject to continuous refinement as Phases 3 and 4 are implemented. Once the *áristos* has been refined into a methodical reverse-engineered sequence of stages, however, the campaign is ready to transition to Phase 3.

---

[157] James Bond, in Ian Fleming's *Casino Royale* (New York: The Macmillan Company, 1953).

Chapter 9: Phase 3

Hour by hour resolve firmly, like a Roman and a man, to do what comes to hand with correct and natural dignity, and with humanity, independence, and justice. Allow your mind freedom from all other considerations. This you can do if you will approach each action as though it were your last, dismissing the wayward thought, the emotional recoil from the commands of reason, the desire to create an impression, the admiration of self, the discontent with your lot. See how little a man needs to master for his days to flow on in quietness and piety; he has but to observe these few counsels and the gods will ask nothing more.
- Emperor Marcus Aurelius, *Meditations* (Book II, 5)

A. Recalling the PhysWar/MindWar Contrast

MindWar Phase 3: Attack is where the entire complex of MW comes together. Everything done previously leads to and integrates at this point, and everything subsequent to it is dependent upon its successful design, coordination, and execution.

A summary of the characteristics of PW vs. MW emphasizes the value of the latter:

1. PhysWar (PW):

- results from the stumbling-into a foreign conflict situation by the United States rather than a discretionary involvement.

- is first preceded by civilian diplomacy which has no clear goal in sight nor strategy to achieve that goal.

- is next preceded by non-DOD paramilitary operations, and/or economic and/or cybernetic damage, none of which has a clear goal in sight or strategy to achieve it.

- is thus the escalation-result of the failure of these two precedent actions, indeed their probable aggravation of the situation.

- consists of the application of lethal and destructive combat force against any appearance of resistance, without concern for the justice of that resistance.

- has no clear goal in sight nor strategy to achieve it. Continued force is simply applied until all resistance ceases, or until disconnected civilian interactions negotiate a suspension.

- utilizes the three old Special Operations Forces - MISO, Special Forces, and Civil Affairs - as battlefield janitors to improve the destructive efficiency of the combat forces and deal with the human and property devastation left in their wake.

- takes an increasingly-larger toll in human injury and death, flight for survival, and enduring hatreds resulting from these.

- diverts massive and increasing amounts of U.S. financial and materiel assets from domestic needs.

- prolongs and aggravates, rather than solves the original problem.

2. MindWar (MW):

- commences as a deliberate, discretionary decision by the United States in concert with all of the participants in the existing problem situation to declare MW against that problem [not one another].

- is preceded by civilian diplomacy aware of a Foundation Diagnosis (FD) developed by MWB, working in concert with MFB towards a stabilizing *áristos*, and planning in concert with PPB for an enduring moral *polis* elimination of the underlying causes of the problem situation.

- in the event of diplomatic failure, commences a military-exclusive MW campaign utilizing the three Special Operations Forces - MWB, MFB, and PPB - as the initial, exclusive projections of U.S. power. All PW forces are kept unengaged, for possible recourse only in the event of MW failure.

  •• MWB's function is to develop the FD and to precondition all participants in the conflict to a mental attitude of calm, reasonable, and constructive cooperation throughout the presence of both MFB and PPB in the situation area.

•• MFB's function is to deploy to the situation area, identify and secure the cooperation of all key individuals and group parties to the conflict, and establish the *áristos* with sufficient stability for handoff to PPB.

•• PPB's function is to commence planning for the configuration and implementation of an enduring moral *polis* solution to the underlying destabilizing conditions upon their identification by the FD, then to deploy to the situation area and implement that *polis* solution upon *áristos* stabilization of the area by MFB.

• kills or injures no one, and destroys nothing.

• expends only the normal operating funds for the MWB, MFB, and PPB units involved and deployed.

• Solves not only the immediate problem but, through creation of the *polis*, potential future ones as well.

• Is declared, again by all participants, to formally end once the *polis* is established and PPB withdraws.

B. MW Command (MWC) Location

The MW campaign is controlled from an encapsulated facility, either contracted or if necessary constructed for this purpose. If the problem situation is confined to a single nation-state, the MWC should be located within it unless the existing destabilization is so great as to pose danger to it. In that case the MWC should be located in a nearby country perceived by all participants as neutral.

The "encapsulation" is from an environmental, not a privileged-access standpoint. The contracted or constructed facility should permit MWB to implement and continue a completely-controlled PSYCON atmosphere, such that anyone within it is subjected to every possible calming, cooperative, optimistic, and creative stimulus; and shielded from all possible negative, disruptive, exhaustive, and stress-inducing ones.

The entire complex is, for instance, bathed in *alpha* BWR and complementary magnetic fields. Its air-conditioning is negatively-ionized. The color red appears nowhere, while the color blue predominates. Sharp, angular lines and objects are eliminated or minimized, and all interior spaces and furnishings are arranged to remain beyond CD but within PSD proxemics [as calculated from the culture(s) of the situation participants], etc.

This PSYCON preconditioning is neither cosmetic nor trivial: It is a precisely-constructed conditioning of the mental processes of all within the MWC to enhance their chances for cooperative success in the campaign. Additionally, while none of these MWB controls is clandestine, they should all be as inconspicuous as possible, so that awareness of or curiosity concerning them does not divert participants' attention from the campaign at hand.

C. MWC Participation

In Phase 0 the MFB begins the process of identifying all participant individuals and groups to the conflict. This identification is refined during Phases 1 & 2 to single out the most essential political leaders, [para]military commanders, and other key participants (such as religious figures and economic executives). By the end of Phase 2 this is narrowed down to the smallest number necessary and essential to consensus concerning and establishment of the *áristos*. These individuals are then invited to the MWC, where together with the United States they will assume control of the campaign.

Within the MWC the United States presence - consisting initially of MFB and then of PPB - remains at all times advisory, on the principle that disputing parties must ultimately resolve and reconcile their own distances and disagreements. Nevertheless this U.S. advisory function is completely and continuously active, not passive. Initially the MW-combative skills of MFB may be called into play to dispel initial suspicions and tensions which resist the MWB environmental conditioning; these flow into MFB's negotiation function.

As a fully cooperative participant climate emerges, MFB fades imperceptibly away from the MWC to be replaced by PPB. The agenda shifts from the immediate *áristos* stabilization to the permanent moral *polis* construction.

D. MWC Integrity

Success of the MWC, and thus of the entire MW campaign, requires that its actions be open, transparent, and at all times publicly explainable. While U.S. and foreign intelligence agencies may [and doubtless will] pay careful attention to what the MWC discusses, decides, and implements, such agencies are not themselves MWC participants. They are, however, all welcome and encouraged to make their information concerning the problem situation available to all of the participants.

E. The On-Site Environment

While the MWC participants are working towards the *áristos* and *polis* realizations, MWB extends the PSYCON atmosphere within the MWC facility to the entire situation area as fully as technology and opportunity permit. This may include use of all EMS media impacting the area to transmit *alpha* BWR, or in extreme instances of violence, *delta* BWR. Negative atmospheric ionization may be enhanced by various weather-control measures such as cloud-seeding. Locales identified as especially susceptible to outbreaks of violence may be measured for disruptive EMFs, and any such detected violence neutralized by either eliminating the source (as in nearby power-lines or unshielded EM-generators) or counterbalanced by directed EMFs.

Obviously PSYCONs extend only so far into a situation of human unrest. Where physical privations of nourishment, safety, health, and cultural lifestyle exist, MFB teams work with all available local, national, nongovernmental organization (NGO), and United States assets to cooperate towards the *áristos* stabilization.

F. MWC/On-Site Communication

MWC participants must at all times know what is happening in the situation area, not only so that they may refine their efforts accordingly, but also because as key leaders and determinants of the social forces in motion they will be reluctant to distance themselves from these forces unless assured that their control and influence are not being severed.

Similarly the situation-local entities and groups must retain a sense of involvement with their leaders, so that their MWC-absence does not result in factionalism or spontaneous disruptions.

G. MWC Transition to On-Site

The purpose of setting up the MWC is to enable swift, efficient actions towards the FD-established *áristos* by all essential participants in an environment PSYCON-engineered for maximum cooperation.

While the MWC facility is also used for initial discussion and planning of the subsequent moral *polis* under the guidance of PPB, the implementation of this *polis* must necessarily occur on-site. Thus as soon as there is basic consensus concerning the nature and structure of the *polis*, which may be markedly different from the existing, haphazard political and social mechanisms, participants return to their original locales to continue the implementation. They are accompanied by appropriately-specialized PPB teams [at this stage MFB's task is done, and it vanishes as magically as Miss Poppins], while MWB continues its conditioning of the entire subject area until the *polis* is securely established and all PPB teams return home.

When all participants have departed the MWC, it remains open only as a point of coordination between the on-site PPB teams and the situation-locational MWB environmental conditioning. As soon as these cease, the MWC is closed, and the MW campaign comes to an end in Phase 4.

Chapter 10: Phase 4

[In response to "Conan, what is best in life?"] "To crush your
enemies, see them driven before you, and hear the
lamentation of the women!"
  - Arnold Schwarzenegger, after Genghis Khan (1162?-1227)

The only victories which leave no regret are those which are
gained over ignorance.
                      - Napoleon Bonaparte (1769-1821)

A. MindWar Victory

Victory in a MW campaign is declared when it has
successfully resolved its problem situation without having
to give way to the PW forces which stand ever close at
hand on all sides of the conflict, ready to honor the Great
Khan.

Where the United States' MW forces are concerned,
their victory is also invisib

le. All three of them appear, function, then disappear
"between the raindrops" - particularly MWB, whose
mental manipulations are significantly subconscious.

What MW participants see is ostensibly a U.S.-hosted
conference in which a constructive compromise,
previously elusive, "somehow" materializes to everyone's
adequate, if not complete satisfaction. At the conference's
conclusion, the parties return home to a "coincidentally"
less-violent situation than the one they left a short time
earlier, inspired by a number of new options for
revitalizing their precarious social structures.

B. Time and Space

1. Time

As per Chapter 8.B., MW solutions to current disputes must be oriented to the cyclical or linear timeframes of those affected. If their perception is linear, the solution will be seen as merely temporary; if cyclical, as applicable indefinitely.

In one conspicuous example, Israel visualizes a divinely-commanded linear mandate to its Holy Land, and will be unsatisfied until the entirety is [re]claimed. Palestinians, regarding their inhabited lands as timelessly theirs, neither understand nor accept Israel's inexorable schedule. Because of this time disengagement, attempts to arrange compromises between them are impossible. Only when all parties to an *áristos* understand and accept it in the **same** time-context will it not self-destruct.

Even when immediate participants are synchronous, external or non-nation/state influences may not be. In the Mideast, for instance, Western-linear governments have found themselves confronted by Islamic movements which are unmoved by the asserted time-legitimized sovereignty of present regimes; what matters to them is the timeless propriety of their religious faith. A MW solution to such situations will have to stand the test of religious as well as secular expectations.

Absent coinciding time-arrangements, an apparently-successful MW campaign cannot expect a final, "textbook" victory. Instead a decision will have to be made to either prolong the campaign indefinitely, which, due to the energy required of all three MW branches, would be prohibitive; or acknowledging failure and standing aside for PW.

Realistically the only way to avoid this would be for the asynchronous participants to accept a harmonious, if not exactly identical timeframework. Historical precedents for this are not encouraging, though western European Christianity [after centuries of violent discord] managed something like it in the face of widespread Enlightenment disaffection with Catholicism and the various Protestantisms alike. Linear Marxism, on the other hand, failed to adapt to the greater pressure of cyclical supranational capitalism, and finally disintegrated under it.

2. Space

As also per Chapter 8.B., the nation/state model of sovereignty persists in some parts of the globe while abruptly or gradually disintegrating in others. Signed agreements and idealistic *polis*-models mean little if the human sand beneath them flows away in unrelated directions, into unanticipated new configurations.

These variables are many: tribal, religious, linguistic, racial, economic, sexual, ideological, supposedly-extinct national identity, and possibly multinational-corporate. Nor is only one of these "unconventional" forces at work within various conflict situations, particularly in the more volatile areas of the world.

Within a MW campaign, Phase 3 must identify and include as participants representatives or leaders from any such influential "irregularities" together with the accustomed nation/state officials. This won't make arriving at the FD or its implied *áristos* any easier, but it will make them realistic in implementation.

C. Bigger Ponds, Bigger Fish

By design a MW campaign addresses the most compact situation which lends itself to reasonable isolation. The larger the scope, the more numerous and complex the variables, until the totality becomes unmanageable as well as unsolvable.

The problem of such intentional limitation, of course, is that those larger ponds, with larger fish swimming in them, are still out there. At any point, whether incidentally or intentionally, one or more of them may impact and possibly overwhelm the more compact MW campaign scenario.

Predictably a balance must be struck. The campaign is continued at its manageable level, but a cautious eye stays alert for external surprises. Some of these, such as international financial cycles, can be taken into account as necessary without much extra effort. Others, such as major PW outbreaks, serious disease pandemics, coups, assassinations, nuclear accidents, major weather-disasters, are wild cards which cannot be anticipated. Any can temporarily or permanently disable an otherwise on-track MW campaign. Just as possibly the factors pertinent to that campaign may be unaffected by a calamity which captures widespread public and media attention.

D. Conclusion: In the Shadow of "Old Nick"

Think of it. On the surface there is hunger and fear. Men still exercise unjust laws. They fight, tear one another to pieces. A mere few feet beneath the waves their reign ceases, their evil drowns. Here on the ocean floor is the only independence. Here I am free! Imagine what would happen if they controlled machines such as this submarine boat. Far better that they think there's a monster and hunt me with harpoons.

- Captain Nemo, *20,000 Leagues Under the Sea*

The period ca. 1350-1600, termed the "Renaissance", was characterized by a continuing increase in secular education [with emphasis shifting from the clerical universities to secular courts and academies]. The medieval-era emphasis on logic and metaphysics gave way to revived Classical learning in areas such as language, literature, history, and ethics.

The Renaissance began in Italy due to its strong ties with Classical knowledge, and due to the comparative wealth of the major Italian cities. From 1450 to 1600 a Neoplatonic movement backed by one of the Florentine Medicis gained considerable influence. Plato's works were translated into Latin by 1469.

It was such a climate in Florence that spawned Niccolò Machiavelli (1469-1527), whose pragmatic ideas were to so infuriate the pseudo-pious and hypocritical officials of his time that "Old Nick" would eventually become a pseudonym for the Devil himself. In actuality Machiavelli never advocated evil or depravity; he was a champion of the good and the virtuous. His "evil" reputation came about simply because he pricked the balloons of so many of the predatory and pretentious.

Machiavelli's political philosophy may be summed up thus: Any means, however lawless or unscrupulous, may be justifiably employed by a ruler in order to establish and maintain a strong central government.

The founder(s) of a society must be excused for acts which are inexcusable after the society has been established. The grounds for this initial license are simply the forceful, initial establishment of good qualities and benefits of the resultant society. Examples of such unprincipled founders in *The Prince* are Moses, Romulus, and Cyrus - each of whom attacked and destroyed rivals in order to found the important state in question.

This license was not venial, however. What Machiavelli saw about him was a chaotic world of callous indifference to human privation and suffering, which he characterized as *fortuna*. In his famous commentary *The Prince* he held that it was incumbent upon wise rulers to recognize both appropriate solutions (*necessita*) to *fortuna* and the most effective timing for their implementation (*occasione*). Properly done, this would result in a general state of well-being (*ordini*), which is the practical aim of politics, guided by the ancient Roman tradition of civic virtue (*civitas*). The key to the achievement of these ends is *virtu*: the ability to think intelligently and act resolutely.

Machiavelli never proposed that "ends justify means". The correct quote from *The Prince* #XVIII reads: "Moreover, in the actions of all men, and most of all of Princes, where there is no tribunal to which we can appeal, we look to results. Wherefore if a Prince succeeds in establishing and maintaining his authority, the means will always be judged honorable and be approved by every one. For the vulgar are always taken by appearances and by results, and the world is made up of the vulgar, the few only finding room when the many have no longer ground to stand on."

Machiavelli saw all political history as an interplay between *fortuna* and *virtu*. When *virtu* is held by the many, republics are possible. When *virtu* is held by the few, tyrannies result.

To understand the governing principles of political life, one must examine the **beginnings** of significant political systems. It is the beginning that sets the pattern for a political situation; successive rulers are relative imitations reflecting that beginning. This is the basis for Machiavelli's being called the first **political scientist**, since he sought an explanation of a state in **what it is and has been** rather than in its future goals or ideals.

It is for this reason that the construction of the moral *polis*, as discussed in Chapter 5, is critical to the successful outcome of a MW campaign. A veneer of *virtu* cannot compensate for, nor long survive in a community lacking *civitas*.

Machiavelli may be considered the first political philosopher to base his philosophy solely upon "natural" [as opposed to divinely-inspired] mankind. The "Divine Law" component of Aquinas' four-part, legal universe was irrelevant to his perceptions and prescriptions.

In his *Summa Theologica* St. Thomas Aquinas (1225-74) described the ordering of the universe by four types of law: **Eternal**, the mind of, hence intelligible only to God; **Natural**, which is Eternal Law to the extent that human reason can detect consistencies in it (e.g. "science"); **Divine** as revealed through Christ and the Christian church; and **Human,** which mankind makes in imitation of and towards the "good" perceived in/ revealed by Natural and Divine Law.

Machiavelli contended that since Divine Law is beyond the comprehension of human reason, it cannot and should not be asserted as justification for social systems. Politics, he argued, belongs wholly to the realm of reason, and should be evaluated on that basis alone. "For the manner in which men live is so different from the way in which they ought to live that he who leaves the common course for that which he ought to follow will find that it leads him to ruin rather than to safety." This focus on achievable practicality (the *áristos*) ultimately encourages man to attain dignity by taking complete responsibility for himself.

In thus relegating religion to something metaphorical and optional rather than literal and mandatory in human affairs, Machiavelli followed the lead of William of Ockham (1288-1348) [of later "Occam's razor" fame], who stressed belief in God as a function of pure faith rather than reason, and anticipated the deism of the Enlightenment several centuries later.

Thus Machiavelli, like Plato and Aristotle, sought the *áristos*. Unlike them he limited it to reason and to mankind in its natural state. And he excused all incidental excesses in a state **only if** an ultimate, common good could thereby be more quickly and thoroughly attained.

What this book proposes is to evolve the rationality of Niccolò Machiavelli to the present century: to argue that *virtu* exists in the soul and will of humanity if, as Camus warned, it is not crushed before it can respond to *fortuna*, recapture the *civitas* of the original moral *polis*, and establish *ordini*.[158]

Unlike Machiavelli, we possess the means to undertake this true Quest for the Grail without resort to the sword. MindWar is not just some new uses for old tools in the U.S. Army's venerable inventory; it is an entirely new way of comprehending and grappling with the concept and reality of war in general.

If the reach is ambitious, so are the stakes - which as reviewed in Chapter 1 are human and material costs near or at unendurable extremes. Left to drift into the increasingly more dangerous currents of PW, not just the United States but the planetary population generally faces a dim and discouraging future, indeed far more lethal and terminal than anything George Orwell conjectured when the worst thing he could imagine were three authoritarian but stable superstates.

MindWar is the secret of Captain Nemo's *Nautilus*: no longer a monster to be feared but the crucible of *kalokagathia*.

---

[158] Cf. Chapter 6.C.

Afterword

- by William Henry Anderson, M.D., M.P.H.
       Consulting Neuropsychiatrist
       Washington, D.C.

I appreciate the opportunity to comment on this remarkable manuscript. It represents a "tour of the horizon" of problems of the information environment as they relate to national security affairs. *MindWar* is an innovative, trenchant, and courageous work.

Sun Tzu, often quoted, but seldom seriously studied, reminds us that the supreme pinnacle of the art of war is to win without fighting, or to persuade the enemy of your superior perspective, such that he would wish to join you. This is the goal of MindWar: to make the wisdom of Sun Tzu operational.

In the current political environment, this will not be an easy task. We are asked to presuppose that our leadership be as enlightened as philosopher-kings, or, failing that, at least not beset by the gang of knaves and buffoons who now provide our daily distraction. To place such power as MindWar contemplates in the hands of such men is a fearful idea.

Thus the underlying premise is to work toward the creation of an environment wherein we become better people. This is a worthy goal, and has been a project which began with Plato. The history of Western philosophy has addressed this conflict. Is human nature immutable, causing us to be destined to antagonism and collective mayhem? Or is it possible that this nature is sufficiently malleable, given wise counsel and leadership, to move away from that destiny.

The history of the 20th century does not inspire confidence that we can do that. But this dichotomy will be debated until the eschaton. *MindWar* represents an attempt to look at the problem with fresh eyes. All previous attempts at improvement of human nature have had poor results, with liberty curtailed and misery advanced. *MindWar* joins the discussion.

This volume is a worthy companion to the works of Wayne Hall and Martin van Creveld, representing a serious effort to reformulate intractable and near-mysterious informational conundrums. It is blue-sky thinking, yet retains a practical core. It contains an essential optimism in a field where such perspective is rare.

William Henry Anderson is a retired neuropsychiatrist living in Washington DC. During his active career he worked at Massachusetts General Hospital and Harvard University. He now consults on intelligence and national security affairs. He has published 95 articles in scientific and policy journals. He served with the US Navy as Chief of Neuropsychiatry and Acting Executive Officer, US Naval Hospital, Guantanamo Bay, Cuba, 1971-1973. He has taught courses on the interconnections of biology, psychology, and anthropology at Harvard University from 1984- 2014.

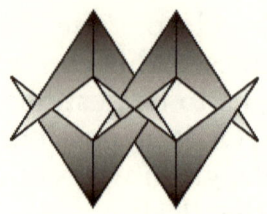

Acronyms

BWR	Brainwave resonance
CA	Civil Affairs/Civil Affairs Branch
CAMG	Civil Affairs & Military Government Branch
CB	Chronobiology
CD	Critical distance
CIA	Central Intelligence Agency
CTL	Command to look
DA	Direct action
DIA	Defense Intelligence Agency
DOD	Department of Defense
EMF	Electromagnetic field
EMR	Electromagnetic radiation
EMS	Electromagnetic spectrum
FD [MindWar]	Foundation Diagnosis
FD [Proxemics]	Flight distance
FID	Foreign internal defense
fMRI	Functional magnetic resonance imaging
IPC	Involuntary psycontrol
JFK	[President] John Fitzgerald Kennedy
LF	Life field
LIPC	Liminal involuntary psycontrol
MACV	Military Assistance Command Vietnam
MACV-SOG	MACV Studies and Observation Group
MEGO	My Eyes Glaze Over (common affliction from reading *MindWar*)
MFB	MetaForce Branch (formerly Special Forces Branch)
MFT	MetaForce Branch Team

MISO	(1) Military Information Support Operations (2) Japanese soup (3) Famous line in the movie *Full Metal Jacket*
MISOC	MISO Command
MKDELTA	Central Intelligence Agency mind-control program
MKSEARCH	Department of Defense mind-control program
MKULTRA	Central Intelligence Agency mind-control program
MONGOOSE	Central Intelligence Agency anti-Castro program
MMS	Magnetospheric MultiScale [NASA mission]
MR	Magnetic Reconnection
MRI	Magnetic resonance imaging
MRP	Magnetic Reconnection Portal
MS	MagnetoSphere
MW	MindWar
MWB	MindWar Branch (formerly Psychological Operations Branch)
MWBG	MindWar Branch Group
MWBT	MindWar Branch Team
MWC	MindWar [campaign control] Command
MWT	MindWar campaign team
NASA	National Aeronautics & Space Administration
NGO	Nongovernmental organization
NLP	Neurolinguistic programming
NSA	National Security Agency
PC (also PSYCON)	Psychological control [method or system]
PhysWar (also PW)	Physical war

PP	ParaPolitics
PPB	ParaPolitics Branch (formerly Civil Affairs Branch)
PRC	Phase response curve
PSD	Personal and social distance
PSYCON (also PC)	Psychological control [method or system]
PSYOP	Psychological operations/ Psychological Operations Branch
PSYWAR	Psychological warfare
PW (also PhysWar)	Physical war
R&A	Research and analysis
SF	Special Forces/Special Forces [Branch]
SLIPC	Subliminal involuntary psycontrol
SO	Special operations
SOF	Special Operations Forces
SR	(1) Special reconnaissance (2) Schumann Resonances
SW	Solar Wind
TF	Thought field
TMS	Transcranial magnetic stimulation
TPJ	Tempero-parietal junction
USA	United States Army
USAF	United States Air Force
USAR	United States Army Reserve
UW	Unconventional warfare
VPC	Voluntary psycontrol

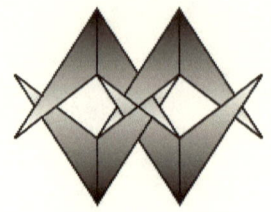

Bibliography

Alexander, Lt. Colonel John B., "The New Mental Battlefield: 'Beam Me Up, Spock'". Leavenworth: U.S. Army Command & General Staff College *Military Review*, December 1980.

Andersen, Per & Andersson, Sven Anders, *Physiological Basis of the Alpha Rhythm*. New York: Appleton-Century Crofts, 1968.

Anderson, William Henry, "Terrorism: The Underlying Causes", *The Intelligencer*. Washington, D.C.: Association of Former Intelligence Officers, 2004.

Anneman, Theodore, *Practical Mental Effects*. New York: Tannen Magic, 1963.

Aquinas, Thomas, *Summa Theologica*. New York: Benziger Brothers, Inc, 1911 (English), 1948.

Aquino, Lt. Colonel Michael A., "Psychological Operations: The Ethical Dimension." Washington, D.C.: National Defense University, 1987.

Ardrey, Robert, *The Social Contract*. New York: Atheneum, 1970.

Army, Department of the, Field Manuals: Washington, D.C.:
3-05.301, *Psychological Operations Process: Tactics, Techniques, and Procedures*, 30 August 2007.
3-53, *Military Information Support Operations*, January 2013.
33-1, *Psychological Operations*, 3 August 1979.
90-2, *Battlefield Deception*, 3 October 1988.

Asimov, Isaac, [in narrative sequence] New York: Doubleday,
Prelude to Foundation. 1988.
Forward the Foundation. 1993.
Foundation. 1951.
Foundation and Empire. 1952.
Second Foundation, 1953.
Foundation's Edge. 1981.
Foundation and Earth. 1986.

Atkinson, William W., *The Will: Its Nature, Power, and Development*. London: L.N. Fowler & Co., 1915.

Aurelius, Marcus, *Meditations*. New York: Penguin Books, 1964.

Becker, Robert O. and Selden, Gary, *The Body Electric: Electromagnetism and the Foundation of Life*. New York: William Morrow, 1985.

Belashchenkow, T., "'Black Propaganda' From Fort Bragg". Moscow: *Sovetskiy Voin*, 1980.

Bloom, Howard, *The Lucifer Principle: A Scientific Expedition into the Policies of History*. New York: Atlantic Monthly Press, 1995.

Burr, Harold Saxon, *The Fields of Life: Our Links with the Universe*. New York: Ballantine Books, 1972.

Camus, Albert, *Resistance, Rebellion, and Death: Essays*. New York: Alfred A. Knopf, 1960.

Carradine, David, *The Spirit of Shaolin*. Boston: Charles E. Tuttle, 1991.

Carrol, Noel, *The Philosophy of Horror, or Paradoxes of the Heart*. New York: Routledge, 1990.

Chandler, Robert W., *War of Ideas: The U.S. Propaganda Campaign in Vietnam*. Boulder: Westview Press, 1981.

Chayefsky, Paddy, *Altered States*. New York: Harper Collins, 1978.

Cleary, Thomas (Trans.), *The Secret of the Golden Flower*. San Francisco: HarperSanFrancisco, 1991.

Combs, James E. & Nimmo, Dan, *A Primer of Politics*. New York: Macmillan Publishing Co., 1984.

Corinda, *Thirteen Steps to Mentalism*. New York: Louis Tannen, 1967.

Cornish, Edward, *Futuring: The Exploration of the Future*. Bethesda: World Future Society, 2004.

Cowie, Peter, *The Apocalypse Now Book*. Cambridge: Da Capo Press, 2000.

Davis, Wade E., *The Serpent and the Rainbow*. New York: Warner Books, 1987.

Dawkins, Richard, *The Selfish Gene*. New York: Oxford University Press, 1989.

de Lafforest, Roger, *Houses That Kill*. Paris: Robert Laffont, 1972.

Deibel, Terry L., *Foreign Affairs Strategy: Logic for American Statecraft*. New York: Cambridge University Press, 2007.

Delgado, José M.R., *Physical Control of the Mind: Towards a Psychocivilized Society*. New York: Harper & Row, 1969.

Drezner, Daniel W., *Theories of International Politics and Zombies*. Princeton: Princeton University Press, 2011.

Dunlop, Beth, *Building a Dream: The Art of Disney Architecture*. New York: Harry N. Abrams, 1996.

Edwardes, Michael, *The Dark Side of History: Magic in the Making of Man*. New York: Stein & Day, 1977.

Elliot, Andrew J. & Aarts, Henk, "Perception of the Color Red Enhances the Force and Velocity of Motor Output". *Emotion*, Vol 11(2), April 2011.

Eisenberg, David & Wright, Thomas Lee, *Encounters with Qi: Exploring Chinese Medicine*. New York: W.W. Norton, 1995.

Eisner, Lotte H., *The Haunted Screen*. Berkeley: University of California Press, 1965.

Ellul, Jacques, *Propaganda: The Formation of Men's Attitudes*. New York: Vintage Books, 1973.

Ferguson, Marilyn, *The Brain Revolution*. New York: Bantam Books, 1975.

Fisher, Roger, William L. Ury, & Bruce Patton, *Getting to Yes: Negotiating Agreement Without Giving In*. New York: Penguin Books, 1983.

Fleming, Ian, *Casino Royale*. New York: The Macmillan Company, 1953.

Fowles, John, Boston: Little, Brown & Company,
   The Áristos. 1964.
   The Magus. 1965.
Gerring, John, *Social Science Methodology: A Unified
   Framework* (2nd Edition). New York: Cambridge
   University Press, 2012.
Green, Ronald E., *The Persuasive Properties of Color*.
   Marketing Communications, October 1984.
Grosser, Maurice, *The Painter's Eye*. New York: Rinehart
   & Co., 1956.
Gykha, Matila, *The Geometry of Art and Life*. New York:
   Dover Publications, 1977.
Hall, Edward T., *The Hidden Dimension*. Garden City:
   Doubleday & Co., 1966.
Hatsumi, Masaaki, *The Way of the Ninja: Secret
   Techniques*. Tokyo: Kodansha International, 2004.
Hersey, G.L., *Pythagorean Palaces: Magic and
   Architecture in the Italian Renaissance*. Ithaca:
   Cornell University Press, 1976.
Herzog, Arthur, *The B.S. Factor: The Theory and
   Technique of Faking It in America*. New York: Simon
   & Schuster, 1973.
Hitler, Adolf, *Mein Kampf*. (Michael Ford Trans.)
   Munich: Verlag Franz Eher, 1935.
Hoban, Jack E., *The Ethical Warrior*. Spring Lake: RGI
   Media, 2012.
Hoffer, Eric, *The True Believer*. New York: Harper &
   Row, 1951.
Hudson, Valerie M., Schrodt, Philip A., & Whitmer, Ray
   D., *A New Kind of Social Science: The Path Beyond
   Current (IR) Methodologies May Lie Beneath Them*.
   Montreal: International Studies Association, March
   26, 2004.
Huntley, H.E., *The Divine Proportion: A Study in
   Mathematical Beauty*. New York: Dover Publications,
   1970.

Iacoboni, Marco, Roger P. Woods, Marcel Brass, Harold Bekkering, John C. Mazziotta, Giacomo Rizzolatti, "Cortical Mechanisms of Human Imitation", *Science* Magazine, December 24, 1999.

The Imagineers, *Walt Disney Imagineering: A Behind the Dreams Look at Making the Magic Real*. New York: Hyperion, 1996.

Iyer, Raghavan N., New York: Oxford University Press, *The Moral and Political Thought of Mahatma Gandhi*. 1973.
ParaPolitics: Toward the City of Man. 1979.

Jaspers, Karl, *Nietzsche*. Tucson: University of Arizona Press, 19065

Kantner, Paul, *Planet Earth Rock and Roll Orchestra*. San Francisco: Little Dragon Publishing Company, 1983.

Keel, John A., *The Eighth Tower*. New York: E.P. Dutton & Co., 1975.

Kissin, Benjamin, "Conscious and Unconscious Programs in the Brain" (*Psychobiology of Human Behavior*, Volume 1). New York: Plenum Medical Books, 1986.

Konner, Melvin, *The Tangled Web: Biological Constraints on the Human Spirit*. New York: Holt, Rinehart & Winston, 1982.

Kripal, Jeffrey J.,
Esalen. Chicago: University of Chicago Press, 2007.
(Ed. with Glenn W. Shuck) *On the Edge of the Future*. Bloomington: Indiana University Press, 2005.

Kurtz, Rudolf, *Expressionismus und Film*. Zürich: Chronos Verlag, 1926.

Lee, Bruce, *Tao of Jeet Kune Do*. Burbank: Ohara Publications, 1975.

Lee, Martin A. & Shlain, Bruce, *Acid Dreams: The Complete Social History of LSD: The CIA, the Sixties, and Beyond* (Revised Edition). New York: Grove Press, 1994.

Lemezma, Marc, London: New Holland Publishers:
Mind Magic. 2003.
Mind Tricks. 2007.

Lilly, John C., *The Deep Self*. New York: Warner Books, 1977.

London, Perry, *Behavior Control*. New York: Harper & Row, 1969.

Luce, Gay Gaer, *Body Time*. New York: Bantam Books, 1971.

Machiavelli, Niccolò, *The Prince and The Discourses*. New York: Random House, 1950.

Mackay, Charles, *Extraordinary Popular Delusions and the Madness of Crowds*. New York: Harmony Books, 1980 (reprint 1841).

Mandelbaum, Adam, *The Psychic Battlefield: A History of the Military-Occult Complex*. New York: St. Martin's Press, 2000.

Marks, John, *The Search for the "Manchurian Candidate": The CIA and Mind Control*. New York: New York Times Books, 1979.

McRae, Ron, *Mind Wars*. New York: St. Martin's Press, 1984.

Mlodinow, Leonard, *Subliminal: How Your Unconscious Mind Rules Your Behavior*. New York: Pantheon, 2012.

Mortensen, William, *The Command to Look: A Formula for Picture Success*. San Francisco: Camera Craft Publishing Company, 1937.

Murphy, Michael,
An End to Ordinary History. Los Angeles: J.P. Tarcher, 1982.
Jacob Atabet. Millbrae: Celestial Arts, 1977.

Naselaris, Thomas *et al.*, "Bayesian Reconstruction of Natural Images from Human Brain Activity", *Neuron 63*, September 24, 2009.

Nashel, Jonathan, *Edward Lansdale's Cold War*. Amherst: University of Massachusetts Press, 2005.

Orwell, George, *1984*. New York: Harcourt, Brace & Co., 1949.

Oschman, James L., *Energy Medicine: The Scientific Basis*. New York: Churchhill Livingstone, 2000.

Ouspensky, Peter D., *The Psychology of Man's Possible Evolution*. New York: Alfred A. Knopf, 1969.

Penrose, Roger, *Shadows of the Mind: A Search for the Missing Science of Consciousness*. Oxford: Oxford University Press, 1994.

Plato, *The Collected Dialogues of Plato* (Ed. Edith Hamilton & Huntington Cairns). Princeton: Princeton University Press, 1961.

Playfair, Guy and Hill, Scott, *The Cycles of Heaven: Cosmic Forces and What They are Doing to You*. London: Souvenir Press, 1978.

Pollock, Daniel C. (Project Director), *The Art and Science of Psychological Operations: Case Studies of Military Application* (2 volumes). Washington, D.C. Department of the Army, 1972.

Prouty, L. Fletcher, *JFK: The CIA, Vietnam, and the Plot to Assassinate John F. Kennedy*. New York: Carol Publishing Group, 1996.

Randi, James, *Flim-Flam: Psychics, ESP, Unicorns, and Other Delusions*. Buffalo: Prometheus Books, 1982.

Reed, Graham, *The Psychology of Anomalous Experience*. Boston: Houghton Mifflin, 1974.

Roenneberg, Till, *Internal Time: Chronotypes, Social Jet Lag, and Why You're So Tired*. Cambridge: Harvard University Press, 2012.

Roetter, Charles, *Psychological Warfare*. London: B.T. Batsford Ltd, 1974.

Ronson, Jon, *The Men Who Stare At Goats*. New York: Simon & Schuster, 2004.

Russell, Edward W., *Design for Destiny*. New York: Ballantine Books, 1971.

Schneider, Al, *The Theory and Practice of Magic Deception*. Amazon.com: CreateSpace, 2011.

Seese, Major Gregory S., "Science of Influence: A Primer for Psychological Operations". Fort Bragg, N.C.: John F. Kennedy Special Warfare Center & School, 2013.

Sibley, Mulford Q., *Political Ideas and Ideologies: A History of Political Thought*. New York: Harper & Row, 1970.

Somit, Albert, *Political Science and the Study of the Future*. Hinsdale: The Dryden Press, 1974.

Soyka, Fred & Edmonds, Alan, *The Ion Effect*. New York: E.P. Dutton, 1977.

Subcommittee on Health and Scientific Research of the Committee on Human Resources, U.S. Congress, "Human Drug Testing by the CIA, 1977". Washington, D.C.: *Congressional Record*, September 20, 1977.

Taylor, Philip M., *Munitions of the Mind*. Manchester: Manchester University Press, 2003.

Thomas, Donald, *The Marquis de Sade*. Boston: New York Graphic Society, 1976.

Trafton, Anne, "Moral Judgments Can Be Altered By Magnets". Cambridge: *MIT News*, March 30, 2010.

Travers, P.L., *Mary Poppins*. Boston: Houghton Mifflin Harcourt, 1934.

Tzu, Lao, *Tao Te Ching* (Stephen Mitchell Trans.). London: Frances Lincoln, 2009.

Ury, William L., *Getting Past No: Negotiating in Difficult Situations*. New York: Bantam Books, 1993.

Vallely, Colonel Paul E., with Aquino, Major Michael A., "From PSYOP to MindWar: The Psychology of Victory". San Francisco: 7th Psychological Operations Group, 1980.

Vandewalle, G., C. Schmidt, G. Albouy, V. Sterpenich, A. Darsaud, G. Rauchs, P.-Y. Berken, E. Balteau, C. Degueldre, A. Luxen, P. Maquet, D.J. Dijk, "Brain Responses to Violet, Blue, and Green Monochromatic Light Exposures in Humans : Prominent Role of Blue Light and the Brainstem". *PLoS One*, 11/28/2007.

Veith, Liza (Trans), *The Yellow Emperor's Classic of Internal Medicine*. Berkeley: University of California Press, 2002.

Verne, Jules, New York:
Journey to the Center of the Earth. Signet Classics, 2012.
20,000 Leagues Under the Sea ("The Annotated Jules Verne" by Walter James Miller). Thomas Y. Crowell, 1976.

Viereck, Peter, *Metapolitics from the Romantics to Hitler*. New York: Alfred A. Knopf, 1941.

von Harbou, Thea, *Metropolis*. Germany, 1927.

Walker, Morton, *The Power of Color*; Avery Publishing Group, 1991.

Washnis, George J. & Hricak, R.Z., *Discovery of Magnetic Health*. Rockville, MD: Nova Publishing Company, 1993.

Waters, T.A., *Mind, Myth, and Magic*. Seattle: Hermetic Press, 1993.

White, John (Ed.), *Psychic Warfare: Fact or Fiction?* Wellingborough: The Aquarian Press, 1988.

Whitrow, G.J., *The Nature of Time*. New York: Oxford University Press, 1972.

Winkler, Franz E., *For Freedom Destined: Mysteries of Man's Evolution in the Mythology of Wagner's Ring Operas and Parsifal*. Garden City: Waldorf Press, 1974.

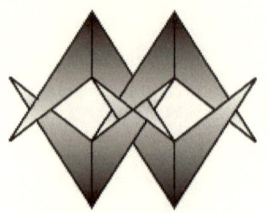

Index

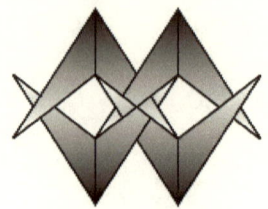

Accessories

For MindWar accessories
please feel welcome to visit:

http://www.zazzle.com/mindwar

... for a gradually-increasing selection of MindWar,
MindWar Branch, MetaForce Branch, and
ParaPolitics Branch raiment and memorabilia.

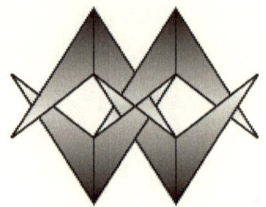

About the Author

After commencing his military career as Cadet Colonel of the Santa Barbara High School Jr. ROTC in 1964, Michael Aquino was commissioned in the Regular Army as a Sr. ROTC Distinguished Military Graduate of the University of California in 1968. After a year with the 1/17th Cavalry, 82nd Airborne Division, he completed the PSYOP Officer Course at the John F. Kennedy Special Warfare School, in which he was among select students cross-trained with the concurrent Special Forces Officer Course.

During 1969-70 he was assigned to the 6th PSYOP Battalion, 4th Group, Vietnam. As an HA Command & Control Team Leader, he was responsible for both tactical (HB) teams in combat operations, and audio-visual (HE) teams in the Civil Operations & Revolutionary Development Support (CORDS) program, and flew numerous PSYOP air support missions throughout III Corps Tactical Zone with both the U.S. Air Force and Army aviation.

In 1972 he joined the 306th PSYOP Battalion (Strategic), USAR at Fort MacArthur, California, and for the next seven years served as Research & Analysis (FA) Team Leader, Operations Officer, and finally Executive Officer. In the 306th - whose members ranged from eccentric Hollywood personalities to dour L.A.P.D. officers - he oversaw highly-classified Basic PSYOP Studies for the Joint Chiefs of Staff, PSYOP support for the training of units such as the 12th Special Forces, and use of the 306th's atmospheric World War II-era bunkers for space combat scenes in the original *Battlestar Galactica* television series.

In 1976 he was selected for the Foreign Area Officer career program, completed that qualification at the Special Warfare Center and Central Intelligence Agency during the next three years, and participated in NATO REFORGER exercises as a Western Europe specialist. In 1976 he also completed the remaining course requirements for Special Forces, and was awarded that Tab upon its creation in 1984.

From 1979 to 1981 he served as the FA Team Leader for Headquarters, 7th PSYOP Group in San Francisco, during which time he and the Group Commander collaborated on the predecessor concept paper to this *MindWar* book.

Returning to active duty in 1981, he was transferred to Civil Affairs Branch, completed its Advanced Course at the Special Warfare Center as the Distinguished Graduate, and received the rare Primary Skill identifier of Politico-Military Affairs Officer (48G). In this capacity he was sent to the State Department Foreign Service Institute and the Defense Intelligence Agency for Attaché qualification, completed the Military Intelligence Officer Advanced Course at Fort

Huachuca, and in 1986 was reassigned to Military Intelligence Branch.

In 1986-7 he was the sole USAR officer selected to attend the Industrial College of the National Defense University. During that year he worked with the U.S. Information Agency representative at the National War College on the *PSYOP Ethics* paper which is also a predecessor to this book.

In 1990 as one of the Army's first officers to be certified in Joint Space Intelligence by the U.S. Air Force, he was assigned to J2 HQ U.S. Space Command, where in Section X, out of the Cheyenne Mountain NORAD complex, he was involved with those files until he retired from the Active USAR in 1994.

Since the Army had waited until the exact date of his final USA retirement 2006 to create the PSYOP Branch, it graciously transferred him "posthumously" to the Green & Grey in 2011. He has retained his original affiliation with the 1st Special Forces Regiment out of respect for that unique honor.

American decorations include the Bronze Star, Meritorious Service Medal, Air Medal, three Army Commendation Medals, two Army Reserve Achievement Medals, Parachutist Badge, Special Forces Tab, and USAF Space & Missile Badge. Vietnamese decorations include the Gallantry Cross, Psychological Warfare Medal, and Air Service Medal.

Academically he received the Ph.D. in Political Science from the University of California in 1980 and the M.P.A. in National Resource Management from George Washington University in 1987. He taught as Adjunct Professor of Political Science at Golden Gate University 1980-86.

Professionally he is a member of the Special Forces, PSYOP, Civil Affairs, Former Intelligence Officers, and Air/Space/Missile Defense Associations.

He is a past National Commander of the Knights of Dunamis (Eagle Scout Honor Society) and recipient of its Knight Eagle Distinguished Service Award. He has also received the Vigil Honor of Scouting's Order of the Arrow, and the Distinguished Service Key of Alpha Phi Omega Fraternity.

He is a Priest of the ancient Egyptian god Set.

After the conclusion of his U.S. government service, the Constitution permitted him to be recognized by Scotland's Lord Lyon King of Arms as the current Baron of Rachane, Argyllshire. He, Baroness Lilith, and inevitable, immortal cats live in San Francisco.